Drop Your Nets and Follow Jesus

Drop Your Nets and Follow Jesus

How to Form Disciples for the New Evangelization

Susan Muto

New City Press
Hyde Park, New York

Published by New City Press
202 Comforter Blvd.,
Hyde Park, NY 12538
www.newcitypress.com

©2019, Susan Muto

Cover design and layout: Miguel Tejerina
Cover photo: Quang Nguyen Vinh

Library of Congress Control Number: 2019943993

Drop Your Nets and Follow Jesus
ISBN: 978-1-56548-685-0 (paperback)
ISBN: 978-1-56548-686-7 (e-book)

Printed in the United States of America

Table of Contents

Prologue

The chief task of discipleship from the time of Jesus until today is to seek out and welcome those who have no faith or who have faltered in their beliefs and moved away from God. Disciples reach out to those who practice their faith and desire to deepen it as well as to those who keep the faith but who realize that for whatever reason their heart has grown indifferent or lukewarm.

The aim of discipleship is to help us deepen our relationship with Jesus so that we can share his love and forgiveness with the world. Disciples focus not only on personal conversion but also on helping their faith community become a vibrant center of worship and service. Such witnessing is less a matter of preaching and more of being present in simple yet convincing ways to the truth of the Gospel. Examples include becoming more patient with an elderly person or helping a child with a learning disability.

Our lives for the most part are as ordinary as Jesus' life in Nazareth must have been. We awaken in the morning, prepare breakfast, go to work, drive home, eat supper, do chores, and get ready for bed. Our lives hardly seem to be a paragon of evangelization, and yet, when we do these ordinary tasks with love in our hearts for the Lord, we excel as his disciples, whether we realize it or not.

When Mary Magdalene approached the tomb on that first Resurrection day, she did not understand why it was empty. She saw someone whom she thought was the gardener; she asked him where they had put her Lord. Only then did Jesus reveal who he was and commission her to go and tell this news to the apostles.

"Go and tell." This divine directive leads us to reflect on what it means in today's world to be *called*, *committed*, *consecrated*, and *commissioned* disciples of the Lord.

When Jesus chose someone to announce his Resurrection, he did not name a woman of noble birth or a person who had lived a perfect life but Mary Magdalene, a woman who, because she recognized her sinfulness, had asked for forgiveness and accepted the grace of conversion. She loved him so ardently that he knew he could entrust to her the first revelation of the Resurrection with its promise of eternal life.

To be *called* by Christ means to be ready to respond to the unexpected—as when he told Simon Peter that he would not catch fish anymore but people.

To be *committed* to Jesus is to remain faithful to our call in the here-and-now circumstances of daily life. In the exchange of marriage vows, a couple promises to stay wed for richer and poorer, in sickness and in health, until death sunders them apart. Such a commitment helps us to grasp the full meaning of what it is to let go of our own agenda, to take up the cross of self-denial, and to follow Jesus in times of joy and suffering. In the words of one of the most committed disciples of our era, St. Teresa of Calcutta, we, too, say, "I am not here to be successful but to be faithful."

To be *consecrated* is to be set apart as witnesses to the Gospel and to see our lives as a response to God, whether we are attending Holy Mass or simply preparing a festive meal for our family and friends.

To be *commissioned* is to gather up the fruits of our called, committed, and consecrated lives for the sake of proclaiming to anyone with ears to hear that Jesus Christ is Lord. Now our entrance to the new evangelization makes perfect sense. We are to grow in spirit, heart, body, mind, and will for the sake of renewing his Bride, the Church, in this time of transition to the third millennium.

There is no better way to facilitate the new evangelization than to try our best to live what we profess to believe. When the Christ in me meets and greets the Christ in you, openings to grace always reveal themselves. To listen with empathy to another person provides an excellent starting point for evangelization. To be a good listener is to be a good evangelizer.

Our life with Christ and in the Church has as its center of gravity the celebration of the Eucharist. Worthily received, it strengthens us to go forth and bring Christ to a world hungering for the wholeness and holiness only he can bestow upon us.

The more zeal we feel, the more abandoned to God we must become. The work of evangelization is not ours to perform; it is a response to God's grace working in and through us for the benefit of others. Saving souls is God's work. Our role is to pray unceasingly and to cooperate with grace. Zealous laboring for souls must be accompanied by absolute abandonment to Divine Providence.

To believe in the power of faith, we must seek the company of faithful people, knowing that in Christ we are connected to one another on all levels of our being. Evangelization is relational because the Master told us that we are our brothers' and sisters' keepers, friends of God who must befriend one another.

Any task God asks us to fulfill in the realm of evangelization can never be accomplished without ceaseless prayer. Through praise, petition, intercession, and adoration, we remain present to the Divine Presence as the deepest ground of our being and doing.

The more we try to witness to our faith with honesty and courage, the more captivating it may be to others. A perennial obstacle to witnessing to the truth of the Gospel is the fear of what others may think. Perhaps that is why Jesus told his disciples not to be afraid (cf. Mt 10:26-27).

Change of any sort, be it inner or outer, disrupts our comfort zone. We would prefer everything to stay the same, packed in the neat box into which we have placed the members of our family and our church, but that is simply not possible. God's way with us is to reform any tendency toward complacency and to transform us into true disciples.

Once we face our fears and misgivings, we are free to behold with a sense of wonder how much God loves and cares for each of us and why spreading the truth of his Word ought to be the centerpiece of our life. We may enter into this Great Commission hesitantly—as a new swimmer may test the water—but soon we surrender to the buoyant lift of grace and shed the barnacles of distrust.

If God has found us worthy to be his servants, how can we refuse to obey his bidding? Knowing that untested faith only grows weaker gives us the courage to put our uncertainty behind us and look to the future with hope.

My reason for writing this book dedicated to forming disciples for the new evangelization is twofold: to uncover the deepest dynamics of what it means to follow Jesus and to help every reader in his or her own way to transform the world into the house of God. Aiding me in this endeavor are the staff and faculty of the Epiphany Academy of Formative Spirituality and many friends and family members, who long, as I do, to make our hearts the dwelling place of the Divine and to hasten the coming of God's reign on earth.

Chapter 1

Dying and Rising with Christ

Epiphany of Mystery
Adrian van Kaam[1]

Epiphany of mystery
Silently embracing
Emergence of creation,
Transforming humanity
By gracious pervasion.
Mystery of gentle grace,
Illumine our ways,
Disclose the eternal exit
From the cage of time,
The empty, trying days,
A caravan of tired camels.
Eternal spark within
Pierce the dreary winter
Of forgetfulness of the Divine.

Clean the clouded window,
Weave threads of light
Through our nights.
Make us risk
The mysterious voyage
Of light and love.
Lighthouse, guide
Our little ships

Tossing on the churning
Waters of history.
Keep afloat the battered barques
Of fleeting lives.
Make us celebrate
Your presence in the depths
Of our being.

Discipleship is meant by God to be the fullest expression of the dying and rising of Jesus. There is no other road to lasting peace and freedom than that which stretches from the suffering on Golgotha to the unspeakable splendor of Easter morning.

The Resurrection of our Lord Jesus is not simply a historical event but a here-and-now reality revealing that Christ is with us always.

From the moment of baptism, our existence becomes a participation in the life of the Trinity. And yet, we confess in humility that there is in our fallen condition a fundamental egoism impossible to overcome without the grace granted to us by our Redeemer. There is a narcissistic bent in our personality that threatens to dismantle our call to selfless love as disciples of and evangelizers for the Lord.

Even at privileged moments of deep listening to what our Master teaches, our inclination to self-centeredness does not disappear; it lies in wait like a snake seeking to poison our spiritual perceptions and motivations. Original Sin has caused a woundedness in our soul whose healing takes a lifetime. We may catch a glimpse of the glory Jesus promises to give us here on earth, but only in the life to come will we behold its full brilliance.

Stillness, recollection, and a serenity not disturbed by useless worry sustain our hope. Anxiety is a sign of the invasion of another kind of spirit, that of self-centered preoccupation. Serene self-possession in daily life is the gift the risen Christ wants to give us.

In his appearances to the apostles and disciples after the Resurrection, Jesus shared with them the peace that is his farewell legacy to each of us. The more we are able to still the noise of our selfish needs and surrender to his loving plan for our lives, the more we will be able to model the peace of his presence in every situation.

The awareness that we are on the way to transformation liberates us from prideful attempts to reach perfection in this life. The fullness after which we strive is not ours to attain. Seeking perfection means that we try to share in the perfect love of the risen Lord by being present to self, others, and God in a less egocentric fashion.

The sacramental character of our Christian existence, especially our participation in the Eucharist, grows stronger throughout our life of discipleship. The transformation that took place in our being at the moment of baptism begins to bear fruit in an outpouring of agapic love. What is most characteristic of the form of Christ in us is that it affects our awareness of all that we are and do, enabling us to respond to him with the commitment characteristic of true discipleship.

The sacrificial life of the Lord means that we, too, must be ready to let go of our innate narcissism and be more present to the demands of our task. Our resistance to letting go of lingering remnants of unconscious egoism appears when Christ challenges us to depart from the safety zone of routine religiosity. It may feel at first as if we are losing our moorings and, to a degree, that is true. As our Lord's presence begins to permeate our daily existence, we grow less sure of our own self-sufficiency and more in need of intimacy with him.

In liturgy, Word, and sacrament, we encounter Jesus in the ecstasy of his risen glory and in the everydayness of bearing our cross courageously. The result is never a turning away from the world in which we are involved but a turning toward it in obedience to the will of the Father.

When we rediscover the core of our Christian personhood—and who we are meant by God to be—we grow in the conviction that we are not alone. Christ is with us from the inception of life to its natural end. His Spirit graces us with renewed gratitude for the past, restored vitality in the present, and unmitigated hope for the future.

It is not enough to be called; we must put our call into practice. Here are five suggestions for doing so:

1. Participate faithfully in the common ways of spiritual deepening offered to us daily by the Church: liturgy, Word, and sacrament.

2. Gain through prayer and study a deeper understanding of our baptismal heritage through pre-evangelization (if we have been away from the Church); through re-evangelization (if we have gone through

an awakening experience and hunger for more teaching); through a new evangelization (to learn how to become "other Christs" through joyful witness and worship).

3. Connect what we believe (our faith tradition) to everyday life (our formation tradition).

4. Be willing to accept the demands our call to follow Christ makes upon us: to parenting, to a profession, to any other obligation this promise entails and duty dictates.

5. Enter into the deepest meaning of knowing who Christ is and why he must remain the center of our field of presence and action.

Saying yes to our calling in Christ is likely to continue for a lifetime if we face day by day these hindrances and counter them with these helps:

Hindrances

1. Inflating "control-center me" and my functional performance.

2. Impatient pushing against the pace of grace as if I am in charge of everything.

3. Focusing on my limits with feelings of hopelessness.

4. Veering from willfulness to will-lessness.

5. Being driven by time-urgency and over-scheduling.

Helps

1. Trusting selflessly in God's providential plan.

2. Patient presence to what *is* and making the best of it in response to God's grace.

3. Seeing my limits as blessings in disguise that reveal my unique call.

4. Practicing authentic willing oriented to God and to implementing God's will.

5. Taking time for reflection in the light of the peace and joy of Jesus.

Let Us Pray

Thrice Holy God, overshadowing us, your people, called to be holy and to live holistically, gifted to form, reform, and transform the community of faith, sent to serve our sisters and brothers eagerly, tirelessly, faithfully.
Renew our hearts by your grace.

Grant us hitherto unknown depths of prayer and presence, as we offer the witness of love and healing in and through Christ to a world wounded by violence, hatred, and ill will, sick in soul and body because of sin.

God the Father, God the Son, God the Holy Spirit, gather us together as husbands and wives, as fathers and mothers, as children and elders, as friends and relatives, into the embracing, caring arms of Christ crucified.

Through him, help us to shoulder the responsibilities we must carry with and for the Church, into the world.

There we can be found reading God's Word, ministering to youth and adults, holding decision-making positions, and responding wherever you place us to souls hungering for spiritual deepening—offering our trials daily in appreciative abandonment to your providential purpose and design for our lives.

Spirit of fire and light, help us as we strive to build a better world for our children, a world revitalized and renewed by a deepening of faith, hope, and love, a Church recreated in the image and likeness of Christ, now and for all ages to come.

In fidelity to the treasures of our faith and formation tradition, give us a spirit of deep prayer.

Let the cry of our heart be a constant reminder to us of your resurrected presence, giving us the courage to carry on, and the compassion to be messengers of hope and healing in a time of transition like our own.

Teach us, Holy Spirit, to speak with a disciple's tongue!

May the Word we cherish become flesh in us, as we strive to foster the ongoing spiritual formation of all we hold dear.

In Jesus' name, we, though many, say in one voice, Amen! Alleluia! Amen!

For Reflection

- In what ways are you becoming more aware of God's presence in everything, even when, humanly speaking, you are "at your worst"?

- Can you recall a moment when you grasped the deeper meaning of your ministerial call to grow in your relationships with God and others for the sake of the Church?

Chapter 2

Living the Joy of the Gospel

Living Shadows of God's Glory
Adrian van Kaam[2]

You are the pathway
To the mystery of joy
Beyond the plight of pleasure
That steals our consonance.
The sweetness
Of your countenance appears
In a thousand mirrors
Of creation,
In the concentration
Of your glory,
Softening the worry,
Avarice and sadness
Of the dreary night
Of human history....
In the desert of the universe.
We are the living shadows
Of your glory
Cradled in eternal love
Before aeons of evolution
And our fleeting moment
In the course of time.

In her *Essential Writings*, St. Teresa of Calcutta reminds us that to express our gratitude to God is to accept everything with joy. She kept a smile on her lips whether she bathed a dying Hindu or accepted the Nobel Peace Prize. Her heroic virtue radiated the good news at the heart of salvation history.

Joy lasts when gratification passes and satisfaction proves to be unfulfilling. Mother Teresa realized that in both poverty and prosperity our joy must spring from a heart filled with love.

To understand what it means to live the joy of the Gospel, we have to ponder what this virtue is and what it is not. Joy of this depth is not a feeling; it is a state of being. It is the by-product of a loving, cheerful, generous heart, of a will committed to practicing the ministry of the smile under circumstances, humanly speaking, that may be hard to bear and that by all indications should evoke only bitter tears and endless complaints. Joy is a state of being, a "be-attitude," that lasts long after consoling feelings disappear. Joy is not a passing whim but a lasting disposition related to the hope of eternal glory.

The staying power of joy is what makes it an essential component of Christian maturity. As we read in the Letter to the Hebrews, ". . . for the sake of the joy that was set before him [Christ] endured the cross, disregarding its shame, and has taken his seat at the right hand of the throne of God" (12:2).

Such joy does not diminish; it expands. Every other facet of life "shrinks." Our physical body grows smaller as we age; our capacity to produce grinds slowly to a halt; our family members and friends become fewer in number. And yet, in the face of inevitable existential diminishment and the sense of loss that accompanies it, joy can paradoxically increase.

Since joy cannot be confined to bodily limits, it finds its proper lodging in the spirit. To speak of a spirituality of joy is to know from experience that one can move from fear to courage, from procrastination to perseverance, from despair to hope. One can, as Mother Teresa said, "have a life of peace, a life of joy" (Mother Teresa: Essential Writings, p. 104). Even in pain and suffering, "total surrender [in joy] consists in giving ourselves completely to God" (p. 37).

Her image of one being like a ray of sun in a community proves to be true when we are in the presence of a joyful person. We feel warmer; it is as if our world expands. Joy takes us to a higher plane of transcendent presence where we acknowledge in gratitude the countless benefits we have received from God.

It is not uncommon to hear people blessed by the "be-attitude" of joy to describe their hearts as swelling out of their chests. As Mother Teresa observes, "If [we are one with Jesus] then love is there, then joy is there, and we will be the sunshine of God's love . . ." (p. 68).

Finally, joy is not a result of our own effort to manufacture it; it is the flower of the grace implanted in us like a seed we can and must choose to nurture. The truth is, "It is through love of God and of neighbor that one arrives at complete happiness, at total service without limits, thus giving God to others, a God of peace, a living God, a God of love" (p. 75).

In the Farewell Discourse, delivered at the closure of his earthly life, Jesus begs his disciples to enter with him into a mystery of joy beyond what we can understand or words can express: "Very truly, I tell you, you will weep and mourn, but the world will rejoice; you will have pain, but your pain will turn into joy. . . . So you have pain now; but I will see you again, and your hearts will rejoice, and no one will take your joy from you" (Jn 16:20,22).

St. Teresa of Calcutta, like all true disciples, is an embodiment of joy and hope despite the fact that human suffering knows no bounds. This counsel of hers bears repeating daily: "Keep giving Jesus to your people, not by words, but by your example, by your being in love with Jesus, by radiating his holiness and spreading his fragrance of love everywhere you go. Just keep the joy of Jesus as your strength. Be happy and at peace" (p. 122).

When we commit ourselves, as St. Teresa did, to serving God's people with joy, amazing changes happen:

1. We move from egocentric to Christocentric love, inspired by the wonder that God has loved us first (cf. 1 Jn 4:7-12).

2. We seek through prayer and study a deeper understanding of our baptismal heritage.

3. We imitate Christ by cultivating such virtues as compassion, humility, and forgiveness.

4. We remain ready and willing to walk the way of the cross in poverty of spirit and purity of heart.

5. We say *yes* always to what the Spirit asks us by de-

taching ourselves from temptations to infidelity and narcissistic individualism. Instead we obey this scriptural command: "Commit your work to the LORD, / and your plans will be established" (Prov 16:3).

In his famous treatise *On Loving God*, St. Bernard of Clairvaux offers four steps to living in joyful love and service:

1. Consider the second part of the Great Commandment: love your neighbor as you love yourself. This kind of self-preserving love for the gift that we are cannot be neglected. It preserves our sense of dignity and prevents abuse.

2. Then we can move to social love, or love of others. We care for our neighbors for their sake as well as for our own benefit, for example, to enjoy good fellowship, to be with people who know us by name. We begin to shift from self-centered to other-centered love for God's sake, because this is what God commanded us to do. We try to purify our motives for caring—away from seduction or manipulation to loving "with no strings attached."

3. Our commitment to Gospel love and service becomes more prudent. We act with wisdom and discretion, as Jesus did. We want our behavior to benefit others, not just ourselves. We even begin to experience gratuitous love, that is to say, loving God for God's sake.

4. We reach the culminating point in our joyful journey to committed relationships: we love self and

others in response to loving God with our whole spirit, heart, mind, and will. Committed love and service unite with ongoing conversion of heart as we pray "to do the will of him who sent [us] and to complete his work" (Jn 4:34).

As always, it helps to review what opposes living the joy of the Gospel and what helps us to make progress:

Hindrances

1. Substituting "activism" for contemplative action, "busyness" for loving service.

2. Neglecting the spiritual resources needed for the new evangelization.

3. Engaging in joyless duty and performance for public acclaim.

Helps

1. Recognizing the efficacy of the ministry of presence, of being with others in love as well as doing what I can to help.

2. Becoming a reservoir of faith deepening and availing myself of the spiritual disciplines of reading, meditation, prayer, and contemplation.

3. Fostering servant leadership, with a heart full of joy regardless of the outcome of my efforts.

Let Us Pray

God of light, illumining the darkness of our world, we promise you, even as we praise you, that we shall faithfully bear the responsibilities set before us as your disciples. We shall see with compassion and help with affection the wounded ones you send our way.

We thank you for giving us this unique formation opportunity as sisters and brothers bound together in Christ's mystical Body to radiate kindness and mercy, as we offer our gifts of love and service to the world.

God of life, giver of every good and perfect gift, we are thankful for the trust you place in us as we live in joyful witness to your grace, confirming the Gospel vision of a world consecrated to bear fruit that will last.

God of love, let the superabundance of your care seep into every crevice of our world, preventing the erosion and depletion of our zeal, making us effective givers of care, restored and re-filled by the splendor of your resurrected presence.

You are the courage that sustains us, the confidence that compels us to be strong and to carry on as messengers of hope and healing in a time of transition like our own. Keep us humble by reminding us that we rely on you utterly and wholly.

God of justice, help us to accept with docility and dedication the graced responsibility you give us to be your witnesses in this world.

God of peace, help us to spread your Word with joy.

God of mercy, help us to stand at the foot of the cross, in adoration of your redemptive sacrifice for the renewal of the world.

In Jesus' name, we, though many, say in one voice, Amen! Alleluia! Amen!

For Reflection

- People today seek to find a caring faith community where Christians gather to pursue a more mature life in Christ. How can our parishes better fulfill this need?

- What are you doing personally to live the joy of the Gospel and to build up the Body of Christ in your family life, in the Church, and in society today?

Chapter 3

Meditating on the Mystery of Divine Mercy

Candles of Compassion
Adrian van Kaam[3]

Staying with grace is staying with you, my Lord,
The One who refreshes and makes new my day,
Who lessens my fascination with futile things
And awakens me to what only counts.
Keep touching me inwardly until the light of insight
dawns.
Do not allow the flicker of light to die
Before it becomes a living flame consuming me.
Make me treasure the dawn that grows in me,
Make me dwell on the voice that speaks inaudibly,
Make me cherish the moment of illumination,
Attune me to the tender beginnings of your inspiration.
Oasis in the wasteland of my life,
Still the noise of daily chatter
That I may hear anew the murmur of the living
waters
Running through the universe.
Mellow me, refine my receptivity
That I may surrender graciously
To the blessings you bestow on me.
Let me hear your invitation whispered gently like
the rains of spring.

Give me an angel's wing to rise with you,
Eternal Lord,
To light the shadows of this dying earth
With candles of compassion.

Mercy, living and visible in Jesus of Nazareth, is like medicine for our world-weary souls. As Jesus teaches us in the Sermon of the Mount: "Be merciful, just as your Father is merciful" (Lk 6:36). Mercy softens the scars of sin and suffering often hidden under a mask of self-sufficiency. A drive-by shooting occurs. An earthquake kills hundreds of people. Who among us would not long for help from first responders, from an expert medical team, from a delivery of food and water for depleted souls? Who among us is not in need of an abundance of mercy to temper our tendency to be overly judgmental or to speak harshly to wounded souls?

Mercy offsets the devastating effects of destructive cynicism, sly sarcasm, and haughty condescension. It activates such corporal and spiritual works as feeding the hungry and offering those most in need a good word to brighten their day.

Mercy is like a magnet that attracts many other virtues to it. Patience, gentleness, and serenity mirror the compassion shown by friends and servants of Jesus. No matter the occasion, Christ calls us to be instruments of mercy wherever we are—with a widow aching from loneliness, or with a child begging for our attention.

Mercy fosters justice and peace. It renews our hope in the goodness of humankind. It teaches us that we are part of, not apart from, one another.

In this era of the new evangelization, we have to strive daily, with the help of grace, to prune the dead branches of indifference to the plight of others and let new shoots of compassion clear away the debris that obstructs Christ-centered love in our hearts.

In the face of the misunderstandings we are bound to encounter when we proclaim the Word, we need to ask the Lord to heal our misery with the balm of his mercy. When crosses seem too heavy for us to carry, now is the time to trust in the blessed benevolence of the Lord's compassionate embrace.

We can be conveyors of compassion:

1. By participating in the suffering and joy of the human family while distancing ourselves from decisions and actions that are contrary to the truth Christ teaches.

2. By fostering the integration of prayer and the spiritual and corporal works of mercy.

3. By seeking the grace of intimacy with the Trinity as the source of our capacity to be compassionate.

4. By conforming our will to God's in such a depth of loving surrender that we *passively* put up with trials and *actively* do what God commands over and above the call of duty.

5.   By experiencing the outpouring of God's mercy and forgiveness and by letting it transform our love for others until we become one in the Spirit and one in the Lord.

What hinders and helps our becoming instruments of divine mercy?

Hindrances

1.   Secular humanistic outlooks that erode my reliance on God.

2.   Resentment and disenchantment when "my will" is thwarted by the divine Mystery.

3.   Arrogance replacing awe, resulting in the loss of the sense of the sacred.

Helps

1.   Practicing the "little way of spiritual childhood" in complete trust and abandonment to God.

2.   Seeing God's providential plan as the disclosure of what is best for me and for all those entrusted to my care.

3.   Abiding in awe-filled attention to the still, small whispers of the Divine.

Let Us Pray

Lamb of God,
When I grow weary with the strain of work or high stress,
Guide me to sweet meadows of presence,
Lovely oases in wastelands of inhumane worlds.

Gentle Master,
When I feel wounded, lonely, forlorn,
Call me home to fields of grass green, pristine,
Symbols of hope amidst despair, lack of care.

Staff of Life,
When I push against the pace of grace,
Comfort me with your warm embrace, calming as cool breezes,
Waves of welcome peace soft as night air.

Good Shepherd,
When I cannot find words to preach, guide, teach,
Draw forth from my heart truths to console abandoned souls
With blessings flowing like water down slopes of melted snow,
Giving comfort to the lowly,
Courage to the faint of heart,
Peace to the afflicted,
Light to people groping in dark thickets of doubt and despair,
Good news for young and old, lean and spare, all those entrusted to my care.

May I be your minister in friendly homes and for-
eign lands,
Laying hands on those sick in body and in soul,
Making whole the broken, humble-hearted,
Leaving behind the ninety-nine
To seek the lost and tempest-tossed,
Those being born and those at heaven's door.
All this I pray, in your name, O Lord!
Amen.

For Reflection

- Can you recall a time in your life when you had no
  choice but to trust in the mystery of divine mercy
  in order to remain faithful to your call to carry the
  cross in the midst of a crisis?

- What was the situation? What was the outcome?

- Were there any disclosures concerning your life of
  discipleship that became clearer to you because of
  this experience?

Chapter 4

Counsels on Discipleship from a Doctor of the Church

A Song for God
Adrian van Kaam[4]

What makes us strong
Is not our self-same pride
But celebrating day and night
Any sign divine
Resounding in the field of life
You carved out for us so tenderly.

As grapes on the vine
We ripen on the tender stem
Of Bethlehem
Till we become a prism
Through which the glow of Christ's charism

Mellows humanity's malformation,
The stubborn fortification
Of hearts of stone,
Bitter and alone,
Filled with resentment
Till we flow in abandonment

Concelebrating his saving end
For our limping lives.

For all creation is a melody,
A song for God,
A song still open-ended,
An unfinished symphony.

The doctor to whom I refer is St. Thérèse of Lisieux (1873-1897). What makes this recognition given to her by the Church so remarkable is that she lived a cloistered life of obscurity in the Carmelite convent of Lisieux, France. There she wrote her famous autobiography, *Story of a Soul*, soon read and loved throughout the world. She died at the age of twenty-four, was canonized in 1925, and was declared a Doctor of the Church by St. John Paul II in 1997. She also wrote poetry, plays, several volumes of correspondence, and a collection of prayers—a prolific body of work for one so young.

In a poem titled "How I Want to Love," written shortly before her death, she offers us the "how to" of becoming a true disciple of Jesus. She reminds us in her simple yet unforgettable way that before one can lead others to a wholesome, happy, and holy life, one has to be friends with and be befriended by the Lord.

The first stanza reads:

Divine Jesus, listen to my prayer.
By my love I want to make you rejoice.
You know well, I want to please you alone.
Deign to grant my most ardent desire.
I accept the trials of this sad exile
To delight you and to console your heart.

But change all my works into love,
O my Spouse, my Beloved Savior.

Like St. Thérèse, we need to ask Jesus with spiritual boldness to listen to our prayers, all the while knowing that the intention behind them is to please God alone and to make his way our most ardent desire, which is to say, "change all my works into love." Were we to put this petition into action, it might mean: "O my Spouse, my Beloved Savior, I *love* making this bed; I *love* doing this batch of laundry; I *love* having to put fuel in the almost empty tank of my car; I *love* going home to cook this meal." Suddenly, everyday chores are in perfect harmony with the Father's will.

More counsels on how to be a disciple of Jesus come from the second stanza of Thérèse's poem:

It's your love, Jesus, that I crave.
It's your love that has to transform me.
Put in my heart your consuming flame.
And I'll be able to bless you and love you.
Yes, I'll be able to love you and bless you
As they do in Heaven.
I'll love you with that very love
With which you have loved me, Jesus Eternal Word.

While the world craves everything but God to fill up empty souls, Thérèse directs her longing to Jesus. She wants the flame of his love to consume her wayward ways so that at all times and in all places she will be able to harmonize her earthly life with the heaven she soon will enter. The medicine she offers to world-weary souls is the healing power of her Master's mercy. Her counsel culminates in stanza three:

> Divine Savior, at the end of my life
> Come get me without the shadow of a delay.
> Ah! Show me your infinite tenderness
> And the sweetness of your divine gaze.
> With love, oh! May your voice call me,
> Saying: Come, all is forgiven.
> Come rest on my heart, my faithful spouse.
> You have greatly loved me.

Thérèse embraced a gentle lifestyle in a daily round of challenges. She overcame discouragement, practiced inner and outer silence, and showed the strength not only to do what her rule required but also to endure endless suffering. She saw the ordinary, not the extraordinary, as the arena in which to answer the call to holiness. According to Thérèse, our littleness characterizes our true condition and puts us in our rightful place before God, for to be little personally means to be humble spiritually; it is to acknowledge that we possess nothing ourselves and that everything comes to us from God and through his Word in Holy Scripture.

> I look upon myself as a weak *little bird*, with only a light down as covering. I am not an *eagle*, but I have only an eagle's EYES AND HEART. In spite of my extreme littleness I still dare to

gaze upon the Divine Sun, the Sun of Love, and my heart feels within it all the aspirations of an *Eagle*. . . . O Divine Word! You are the Adored Eagle whom I love and who alone *attracts me*! . . . Eternal Eagle, You desire to nourish me with Your divine substance and yet I am but a poor little thing who would return to nothingness if Your divine glance did not give me life from one moment to the next. (*Story of a Soul*, Chapter IX)

Participating in spiritual childhood implies a willingness and a desire for humility—a desire to be small—in order to be lifted up to God. For Thérèse, the essential quality of the Divine Heart is the humility in which it is "emptied"—poured out—as St. Paul elucidates in Philippians 2:5-7: "Let the same mind be in you that was in Christ Jesus, / who, though he was in the form of God, / did not regard equality with God / as something to be exploited, / but emptied himself . . ." Thérèse recognized that this was the hallmark of God's love for us, and thus she believed that it must also be the governing principle of our love-response to God.

Thérèse teaches that any apostolate is most efficacious when one turns one's face fully toward the Lord, realizing that on one's own one is too insignificant to assist anyone. Consider this description of her sense of helplessness when she received the assignment to serve as mistress of novices:

> Lord, I am too little to nourish your children;
> if you wish to give through me what is suitable
> for each, fill my little hand and without leaving
> Your arms or turning my head, I shall give Your
> treasures to the soul who will come and ask for
> nourishment. (*Story of A Soul,* Chapter XI)

Thérèse realized that the Church is a Mystical Body composed of diverse cells or members and inspired and enlivened by the Holy Spirit, who gives life and energy to all its members. In this light, she clarified her own vocation: since love is everything and contains all vocations, she could hold only one vision and one aspiration: to love, and to inspire others to love God. This was the equivalent of all other apostolic labors and all vocations:

> I understood that if the Church had a body
> composed of different members, the most
> necessary and most noble of all could not be
> lacking to it, and so I understood that the
> Church *had a Heart and that this Heart was
> BURNING WITH LOVE. I understood it was
> Love alone* that made the Church's members
> act, that if *Love* ever became extinct apostles
> would not preach the Gospel and martyrs
> would not shed their blood. I understood that
> LOVE COMPRISED ALL VOCATIONS,
> THAT LOVE WAS EVERYTHING, THAT
> IT EMBRACED ALL TIMES AND PLACES
> . . . IN A WORD, THAT IT WAS ETERNAL!

Then, in the excess of my delirious joy, I cried out: O Jesus, my Love . . . my vocation, at last I have found it. . . . MY VOCATION IS LOVE! Yes, I have my place in the Church and it is You, O my God, who have given me this place; in the heart of the Church, my Mother, I shall be *Love*. Thus I shall be everything, and thus my dream will be realized. (*Story of A Soul*, Chapter IX)

Sick as she was toward the end of her life, Thérèse knew that God's great love for her would cast out all her fear. She relies, in her passing away, on the infinite tenderness of her Savior. She begs to behold the sweetness of his gaze and to hear him call her name. Her final prescription for holiness can be summarized in one word: "Come." Perhaps she remembered how Jesus chose this word to foster the essence of discipleship: Come and see. Come, follow me. Come away to a deserted place and rest a while. "Come to me, all you that are weary and are carrying heavy burdens, and I will give you rest. . . . For my yoke is easy, and my burden is light" (Mt 11:28,30).

To these wondrous appeals, this Doctor of the Church adds two of her own: "Come, all is forgiven" and "Come rest on my heart." That is her formula for following Jesus as all faithful disciples must do: loving him wholly because he has first loved us.

Let Us Pray

Lord, I hear you whisper in my soul: Remain in me, then I will remain in you (cf. Jn 15:4-7). Your loyalty to me, my Lord, can never be questioned. You are fidelity itself. You loved me and pruned me before I could love you. Your acceptance of me is not hemmed in by impossible conditions. You are all for me even when I am against you. You cherish me no matter how I feel or am. It is only I who can be unfaithful to you. Therefore, you have to say: "Remain in me." You assure me once and for all: "Then I will remain in you."

How direct and simple is the promise of your presence. You don't tell me that it is anything out of the ordinary. It is not a question of elated experiences. They may or may not accompany your presence in me. Your presence is not only for people more exalted than I, people unusually graced and gifted. It is also for me, a simple believer in your daily love and care.

To remain in you is not a feeling or a feat of perfection. To remain in you is to believe in you, to surrender to you in faith, hope, and love. When I ask to remain in you, I ask for a special dimension of the grace of faith, the dimension of fidelity. Please, Lord, let faith and fidelity abound in me; let them fill the empty spaces of my life.

Amen.

For Reflection

- Have you ever felt, as St. Thérèse did, that you are far from being a saint and all that counts for God is living in love?

- How did you come to accept that what was—painful as it may have been—was God's gift to you?

- How has St. Thérèse's story helped you to become more aware of the presence of God in everything, more convinced than ever that, in her words, "everything is grace"?

Chapter 5

Obeying the "Little Commandments" in the Gospel of John

Worship of You Alone
Adrian van Kaam[5]

Thank you for beseeching me
To bend my knee
To bow before your blazing throne
To give my heart to you alone.

My spirit, mind, and loving will
Light up like candles white and still
Venerating Father's will.

Unwind my restless mind,
Remind my aching heart
That from the start
You were merciful and kind
To me, your wayward child,
Who did abide in foolish pride. . . .

In days of darkness
When hope grows dim,
You refresh my tired soul,
You show me how to cope
With my despair.

Recall then your care,
Your pledge of leniency.
You wipe away so tenderly
My stream of tears.
You soothe my sorrow
Opening up a new tomorrow,
With snow as white
And bright as laser light.

Above all, my Adored,
Bind me with the shining cord
Of love that takes away
The sting of sin, the cruel play
Of frigidness, tepidity.
Transforming me into a worshiper
Of only thee, O Holy Trinity.

If asked to recite the Great Commandment, we would say without hesitation: love the Lord your God with your whole heart and soul and love your neighbor as you love yourself (cf. Mt 22:37-39). It might be relatively easy for us to remember the Ten Commandments in the Old Testament and the eight Beatitudes in the New Testament too.

What we overlook, however, are the "little commandments" given to us by Jesus to lead us from superficial ways of following him to the depth dimension of lifelong discipleship. The command Mary gave to the wine stewards at the wedding feast at Cana strikes us as one all of us must obey: "Do whatever he tells you" (Jn 2:5).

Inspired by this directive, we can read in the Gospel of John what happens to us when we enter into a person-to-Person relationship with the Lord of Love and through him with the Father of Light and the Spirit of Truth.

Of the many imperatives exemplified in the Gospel of John, there are nine that merit our attention here. Among the most consoling is the first: *"Do not be afraid"* (6:20). Fear understandably grips us when Jesus asks us to follow him into the unknown land of lasting fidelity. Because we do not know for sure where he will lead us, we might be tempted to take a "better safe than sorry" stance toward life instead of following the prophetic path Jesus invites us to pursue.

A second word of truth comes after Jesus feeds the five thousand and his disciples ask him candid questions about why he has come among them. He has to correct the assumption that he came only to feed them when they were hungry, commanding them gently but firmly: *"Do not work for the food that perishes, but for the food that endures for eternal life, which the Son of Man will give you"* (Jn 6:27). Think of how much time we devote daily to what will never last anyway. How different our lives might be were we to obey this second little commandment and focus as much as possible on what lasts, beginning with the Word of God himself.

Here's another striking directive: *"Do not complain among yourselves"* (Jn 6:43). Of course, the disciples are debating about what this bread from heaven really is, but the implication of this imperative extends to the habit we may harbor of complaining about everything. Muttering. Grumbling. Whining. Just listen to the chatter around the coffee machine and imagine what it might be like to go through life without complaining: thanking God for all that is; walking in the light of Christ's presence; offering compliments rather than condemnations.

In the encounter between Jesus and the woman caught in adultery, we find the fourth imperative, one of his most powerful. It ought to be etched on each of our hearts and arouse the compunction that directs us to seek the sacrament of reconciliation: *"Go your way, and from now on do not sin again"* (Jn 8:11).

When Jesus revealed himself as the Lord of life, when he raised Lazarus from the dead, he said four startling words to those who followed him: *"Take away the stone"* (Jn 11:39). He meant the barrier blocking the tomb where his friend had been buried, but if we apply this brief command to our own life, it may mean to remove whatever stands between us and God. What is it that makes us so stubborn and hard-hearted? Is it the stone of unforgiveness? Then it must be taken away. Is it the stone of harsh judgment? Then remove it, for the Lord of life wants to unbind us as well. He has come to set us free.

After he washed his disciples' feet at their last supper together, Jesus gave them a sixth imperative, the new commandment they must obey if they dare to call themselves his friends: *"Love one another. Just as I have loved you, you also should love another"* (Jn 13:34). Such other-centered love, freed from the trap of self-centeredness, is *the* mark of discipleship. There is no ambiguity about it: either we love one another as Christ has loved us or we separate ourselves from him.

Following this core directive of discipleship, Jesus offers three more "little commandments." It is important to note that all three of them are relational. They draw us to become friends of Jesus, not to follow him merely outwardly but in the way of knowing that only comes from true intimacy. Thus he says: *"Abide in me as I abide in you"* (Jn 15:4). *"Bear much fruit and become my disciples"* (15:8). *"Ask and you will receive, so that your joy may be complete"* (16:24). Abide . . . bear fruit . . . receive. These are not only commandments to follow; they are promises upon which we can and must rely. Jesus himself orders us each day to listen to him and thus to be transformed, saying:

> If you love me, you will keep my commandments. And I will ask the Father, and he will give you another Advocate, to be with you forever. This is the Spirit of truth whom the world cannot receive, because it neither sees him nor knows him. You know him, because he abides with you, and he will be in you. (Jn 14:15-17)

Rather than associate obedience with harsh methods of mortification, we ought to foster a master-disciple relationship, rooted in our willingness to obey the Word of the Lord. No commission we receive can be fulfilled unless we link this discipline with discipleship:

> Endure trials for the sake of discipline. God is treating you as children; for what child is there whom a parent does not discipline? If you do not have that discipline in which all children share, then you are illegitimate and not his children. Moreover, we had human parents to discipline us, and we respected them. Should we not be even more willing to be subject to the Father of spirits and live? (Heb 12:7-9)

The Letter to the Hebrews goes on to explain that our parents discipline us at the right time and in accordance with what they deem best for the family unit. God disciplines us for our own good so that we may share in the life of holiness that signifies our covenant of friendship. The discipline asked of us may often seem more painful than pleasant, but "later it yields the peaceful fruit of righteousness to those who have been trained by it" (12:11).

An exemplary discipline emblazoned on the hearts of servants of the Lord is obedience. Because he has chosen us to live by and witness to his Word, despite our limitations, we beg for the grace to listen. Because the Almighty has bestowed such a great favor upon us, we feel empowered to stand up for what is right in every situation without falling prey to anxiety or ego-exaltation. What we do is not merely another duty to be accomplished in a long string of endless projects; it is a way of seeing every endeavor assigned to us by God as another chapter in the book of how to form disciples for the new evangelization. The disciplines we embrace, from spiritual reading to serving our neighbor, stem from the desire to be and to become better listeners to the Gospel directives we have received.

The Apostle Peter reminds us that disciples and friends of God must remain vigilant because "like a roaring lion your adversary the devil prowls around, looking for someone to devour" (1 Pt 5:8). Reading God's Word and meditating upon it, praying unceasingly, and practicing charity are spiritual exercises that ready us to resist demonic seduction and secure the reign of God on earth.

Let Us Pray

Lord, lead me away from the trap of superficial piety devoid of care for others.

Grant me a small portion of the truth, known to all saintly people, that other-centered love is the chief discipline of discipleship.

In response to your grace, let me become your servant in this world without becoming its slave.

Take me with you into the desert of discipline that I may be found worthy to be sent forth into this world as an ambassador of your mystery (cf. 2 Cor 5:20).

Amen.

For Reflection

- How can you grow more sensitive to what Christ asks of you on a day-to-day basis, that is to say, how can you place listening—obedience—at the forefront of discipleship?

- Are you still and quiet enough to hear the Holy Spirit speaking in your heart and in the midst of your ordinary, everyday circumstances?

- What causes you to resist the Spirit's commands? What most helps you to cooperate with them?

Chapter 6

Going into the Vineyard of Evangelization

Jesus the Prophet
Adrian van Kaam[6]

Thaw the tundra of my soul,
Uproot the weeds that choke your gift.
Till the soil, dig the furrows
In which your grace may softly sink
To weather the winter of my heart.
Do not allow your grace in me
To dwindle like seed
Choked off by weeds
That suffocate and drain its power.
Let me gather sweetness from your flowers
In the garden of my soul.
Let my ear remain attuned
To your silent voice of Love
O prophet of my destiny,
O infinite sea that carries me.
Let my life flow forth
From your prophetic call
In the still point of my soul.

"When he went out about nine o'clock, he saw others standing idle in the marketplace; and he said to them, 'You also go into the vineyard'" (Mt 20:3-4).

The command to go into the vineyard places evangelization in the context of both the universal call to holiness and the ministerial response the Lord expects of us. Every believer must obey the command: "You also go."

Christian discipleship is a process through which we are formed by the Father, reformed into the image of the Son, and transformed through the guidance of the Holy Spirit. Fully immersed in this dynamic process of formation, reformation, and transformation, we become better equipped to give testimony of the reason for the hope that is within us (see 1 Pt 3:15).

We need to hear the invitation to go into the vineyard of evangelization as if Christ were saying to each of us: "Come away . . . and rest a while" (Mk 6:31). After that, we may begin again, with renewed vigor, to live and act as witnesses to the Gospel.

The initiative for such inspiration rests with God alone. We cannot force it; we must wait in loving attention for its disclosure. Inspiration does not necessarily mean the infusion of new ideas. What comes to us may sound familiar, only now it is alive in our hearts. This attitude of receptivity to the Holy Spirit keeps us awake and on the watch for those moments when "God's Word" becomes "God's Word for me."

As we bow in awe before the Mystery that embraces our life from beginning to end, we ready ourselves to respond to the expected and unexpected events that are part of our faith journey. We do our best to harmonize its unfolding with the challenges placed before us by life in the vineyard of evangelization.

At times we know with surprising clarity what God wants of us. At other times we may only catch glimpses of this or that thread in the tapestry of discipleship. We are free to accept or refuse what we observe, to trust or distrust that toward which we are being led by God.

This goal demands that we tend the vineyard of our call in faith, hope, and love, that we obey the commandments, and that we grow in the life of prayer. Being detached from every expression of selfish sensuality is the best way to *say yes always* to the Lord's invitation to follow him.

It is through formative reading of Holy Scripture and the classic and contemporary masters of spirituality that we begin to remember in faith the never-ending process of our becoming servants of the Word. As we develop and deepen, as we open ourselves more and more to God's grace alive and at work in us, the words we read may be the same, but their meaning is different. The text begins to disclose its secrets to us. Even texts that seemed easy to understand at first glance may become more enthralling. The faith we took for granted challenges us anew.

Hope teaches us that this world cannot offer us lasting rest, that nothing but God can fulfill the restless yearning of our heart. In the light of hope, we are loosened from the things on which our earthly hopes may be glued. We begin to deal with life's gifts in a caring yet detached manner, as stewards instead of owners. We become able to enjoy and praise in thanksgiving the limited goodness, truth, and loveliness of the things that surround us. We see them as pointers to the world awaiting us in the life to come.

To become fully human and truly Christian, love has to be "chastened" or "purified" of self-centered passions and purposes, anxious needs, and over-dependent demands. Only when our love is chaste can we diminish the tendency to use or abuse others only for our own need of fulfillment or ego-enhancement.

Chastened or purified love expresses the appreciative aspect of human love. It is a commitment never to violate the God-given integrity and dignity of self and others. Committed love makes people friends and companions on the road to maturation in the Lord.

To imagine and to image in word and deed how to live chastely and lovingly in the Spirit of Christ takes a lifetime of cooperation with the transforming love of Christ for each of us.

With the help of grace, we can move from egocentric to Christo-centric love. We begin to abandon ourselves into God's hands. We listen to whatever the Vine Grower tells us to do—be it *passively* by our long-suffering through trials or *actively* by making choices that are in harmony with the truths Jesus has taught us. We persevere in humble submission to the Lord, ready and willing to be commissioned by him to go and "make disciples of all nations" (Mt 28:19). Slowly but surely, our life becomes a kind of Eucharist of everydayness, an offering of sacrificial love to the Father through Jesus in the Spirit.

Let Us Pray

Father, aid me in my quest for peace.
Help me to heal the fragmentation of this frantic life.
Let me escape the clutch of my own ego control.
Only then, Lord, shall I find the peace I so ardently seek.

You gave us the words of eternal life.
You taught us how to pray for peace.
Hallowed be thy name, Father in heaven.
May thy kingdom on earth be as real for me now as it shall be hereafter.
May I do your will in this life as I desire to do it in the life to come.

Though I may forget to ask you, sustain me with the daily bread of life that comes to me through the words of the sacred writers.
Though I am unworthy, I ask your forgiveness for the times I have done things against you.
In thankfulness to you for this forgiveness, I shall do my best to extend forgiveness to others.

Most of all, Father, guide me along the path of salvation.
Deliver me from the bondage of iniquity, my own and that of those persons and events that block my passage to you.
Whenever I do get lost, grant me a little light by

which to return to your dwelling place with no further delay.

I ask these favors not because I deserve them, but because I know that without your grace I am incapable of finding my way.

Guided by your light, I can sing your praises with the spiritual masters, bearing a message not of regret but of joy, not of sorrow but of thanksgiving.

Amen.

For Reflection

- How can you simplify your life enough to see what God needs you to do rather than slavishly fostering your own agenda and planting seeds of evangelization on unfertile ground?

- What must you do to bring to the attention of all those entrusted to your care the goodness, truth, and beauty of the divine plan?

Chapter 7

Lift High the Cross

Redeemer of the Earth

Adrian van Kaam[7]

Each small thing you daily do
Within the boundlessness of space and time
Holds a dignity and depth of meaning and effect
You can never fully grasp.
When it all becomes too much for you,
Grow serene enough to listen
To the gentle cadence of my voice
In your open, waiting heart.

Always interweave the grace of inner presence
With the ebb and flow of everyday events.
Fight the battle blest against the blight
Of injustice, famine, war, drug-infested streets,
The weeds of sin
On my defiled and desecrated globe.

Don't despair, rekindle hope
In my redemptive guiding light
Restoring dignity
In crushed demeaned humanity
Endowed with transforming potency
By me, Redeemer of the earth.

The inspiration for the hymn "Lift High the Cross" can be found in 1 Corinthians 1:18: "For the message about the cross is foolishness to those who are perishing but to us who are being saved it is the power of God."

The first stanza of this uplifting song expresses the invitation which we freely accept as followers of Christ. We sing, "Come, Christians, follow where the Master trod." Imagine where that was! Across the Egyptian desert when it was safe for him as a boy to return with Mary and Joseph to Nazareth. Prior to his public ministry, he went into the desert for forty days and nights to prepare for what awaited him. After the wedding feast at Cana, he began to attract seekers around the Sea of Galilee. Three years passed until he had to go to Jerusalem, where he would meet his destiny. Walking the way of the cross would soon be replaced by his triumphant walk to Emmaus.

Are we willing to walk where our Master trod? Across deserts of intense inner purification from the dissipating power of sin? If he calls us, do we have the courage to drop our nets and follow him? That means dropping egocentric ambitions and the comforts of prosperity that might result in our being possessed by our possessions. Will we be ready to deny ourselves and take up the crosses life puts upon our shoulders—from picayune irritations to major devastations? Do we really believe that the cross is our salvation? If the answer is yes, we become able to sing: "Lift high the cross, the love of Christ proclaim, till all the world adore his sacred name."

There is much promise in that phrase: "follow where the Master trod." In John, we read what Jesus said to those early believers: "I am the light of the world. Whoever follows me will never walk in darkness but will have the light of life" (8:12). Jesus' "I am" self-description contains an amazing promise: If we "follow where the Master trod" (from the darkness of Good Friday to the brilliance of Easter Sunday), we will leave the land of unlikeness darkened by sin and walk into the land of likeness to Father, Son, and Holy Spirit, radiant with the light of life, on earth and in heaven.

This text means that we must "walk by faith, not by sight" (2 Cor 5:7). Reason alone would preclude our following a crucified Savior. That is why we need faith—though it be "the size of a mustard seed" (Mt 17:20)—to run the race of discipleship from start to finish. Once again we can raise our voices and sing with all the saints: "Led on [our] way by this triumphant sign, the hosts of God in conquering ranks combine" (stanza 2).

People who allow suffering to raise them up to new heights of nobility usually grow more open, wise, and gentle than those who fight it or flee from it. Their self-understanding enables them to understand and console others. Because they believe that what is happening to them has a definite purpose, they can appreciate more fully the part suffering plays in the overall pattern of human life. They can assure us that with time and reflection the purpose of the cross Jesus asks them to carry will become clear.

When we become more sensitive to the richness of our everyday life, we feel inwardly renewed. We become freer to care in gentle yet firm ways for the persons who rely on us. We try to make each day count for something, whether anyone notices our efforts or not. Behind the apparent dullness of daily life, we discern a deeper meaning. Somehow each passing moment becomes an expression of the eternal. In this way, the crosses inherent in day-to-day existence bestow upon us a profound purpose.

The Christian message sealed the bond between suffering and love, persecution and holiness, trials and trust in Divine Providence. Christians can rejoice in spite of the things that grieve them, for such times of testing are sources of renewed faith, hope, and love; they are part of God's forming mystery for our lives. In fact, no true transformation of heart is possible without them.

If our confidence in Christ is strong, we can cope with these experiences and grow through them. Nothing we have to endure—no pain, insult, or injury—can be as devastating as that which he took upon himself for our sake.

The ashes on our forehead at the beginning of Lent reveal the "seal of him who died" (stanza 3) and the incredible paradox at the root of our faith that this Lord "once lifted on the glorious tree" and condemned to death bought us life eternally (stanza 4). The price he paid defied protocol. Nothing like it had ever happened before—that out of such a vicious end comes eternal victory. What could be more fitting for us to sing, in soaring tones or the softest of whispers: "Lift high the cross, the love of Christ proclaim, till all the world adore his sacred name."

Let Us Pray

Lord, sinful as I am, I know that I can kneel before you and find you awaiting me with love untold.

This gift of love is freely given and by me it must be as freely received.
Such receptivity requires faith in that which is beyond anything this world can offer me.

Grant me the grace I need to find this depth of faith.

Let me experience each day the struggle to find you and, as you will, the joy of being found by you.

Grant that my way may become simply your way for me.

In spite of my unworthiness, let me become a disciple of your Word, filled with the same Spirit the apostles experienced when you looked at them and said, "Come, follow me."

Amen.

For Reflection

- Have you learned to appraise the crosses in your life as disclosures of your calling in the Lord?

- Do you see a formation opportunity emerging in your spiritual life each time you have to bear the cross of Jesus?

- The Apostle Paul says that as Christians we "boast in our sufferings, knowing that suffering produces endurance, and endurance produces character, and character produces hope, and hope does not disappoint" (Rom 5:3-5). Do you boast in your sufferings, rather than allowing such suffering to become a source of bitterness, self-pity, or blame?

Chapter 8

Examining the Truth
of Our Call to Follow Jesus

Meekness of Heart
Adrian van Kaam[8]

Let the splendor of your presence
Light up my everydayness.
Make me a smooth channel for the outflow
Of your Divine Will in this world.
Let me dwell meekly
In the presence of your Mystery.
Harmonize my frail spirit with the infinite Spirit
Who fills the universe and its history.

Jesus, holy, meek, and mild
Make my heart less harsh and wild,
Melt away its stubborn pride.

The Church's invitation to participate in the new evangelization presents each of us with an opportunity to examine the truth of our calling in Christ as lived in the past, sustained in the present, and extended into the future. This call must be embodied in our chosen vocation, for example, as a priest or a religious, a married or a single person. What all of these vocations have in common is the desire to live for Jesus in single-hearted love, inspired by the beatitude: "Blessed are the pure in heart, for they will see God" (Mt 5:8).

Our Lord reveals the blessings that accompany conformity to him. Do we encounter him on distant shores as well as on the highways and byways of life? Do we accompany him to the desert of silence and solitude? Have we vowed to pursue new depths of discipleship and the ministerial excellence it demands?

Single-hearted followers of Jesus, like the virgin-martyrs of old, are passionate witnesses to the art of loving without demanding to receive love in return. To imbibe the wisdom that comes through suffering is a daily challenge, calling for conversion of heart, especially when, as in all relationships, the "honeymoon" of initial consolations gives way to the trials of spiritual dryness.

Obeying our call to follow Jesus casts us into the daily grind of pursuing an education, paying bills, providing for our family, and coping with foes we thought were like-minded friends. Though we are often misunderstood, of this we can be sure: the Lord is nearer to us than we are to ourselves.

In the course of trying to fulfill our call, knowing in part and yet not fully certain where it will lead, we may feel like astronauts lost in the vastness of space, hurtling at astronomical speeds toward a horizon that is constantly receding.

Who among us has not felt threatened—even terror-stricken at times—by the fact that we cannot predict the outcome of following Jesus? What is not predictable cannot be controlled, no matter how hard we try.

The human spirit is like a camera with a complex focusing mechanism. It takes time to bring the full picture into view. We can never predict the exact way God would have us go, nor can we know in detail the kind of guidance we will receive or whence it will come. At times we see with surprising clarity what God wants. More often than not, we can catch only a glimpse of a particular facet, but not the whole view, of our life direction.

God calls us at times to plunge into the unknown depths where love leads. We respond by gathering up our courage and dipping one foot, followed by another, into the cold water of uncertainty.

No wonder we hesitate before committing ourselves to a major step in life like marrying, staying single, becoming a priest or minister, or joining a religious community. Such decisions are never easy to make, but answers can be found with the help of wise guides, good books, and regular prayer.

The same feeling of hesitation may arise when we respond to our call in less momentous matters. We may want to flee from the responsibility imposed on us each day. We may try to escape to some imaginary place of minimal obligations and pleasant companions. We miss the point that spirituality is reality. We cannot reap the rewards of being faithful in the future unless we address the mundane demands of the present.

Whether we forge ahead in foolhardy boldness or tiptoe forward in trepidation, God is with us. Despite the uncertainty we feel, our divine caller will not leave us forsaken. In his farewell address, Jesus assures us: "I will not leave you orphaned; I am coming to you. In a little while the world will no longer see me, but you will see me; because I live, you also will live" (Jn 14:18-19).

In the light of this promise, the pursuit of dedicated discipleship has more than one "not" consequent upon it. It must not be accepted reluctantly as a painful cross to bear with little or nothing about it to celebrate. It must not put us on the defensive as if we are obliged to find a logical set of reasons to justify or explain the mystery of our calling. We must be sure not to deny our dependence on God, lest we curtail further growth in compassion, generosity, and other-centered love.

Joy abounds and peace descends upon us in the realization that to follow Christ goes beyond the confines of any one era. It points to the promise of meeting face to face the Lord whom we adore, and being welcomed by him as good and faithful servants.

Let Us Pray

Lord, show me day by day how to follow you from the Mount of Calvary to the glory of Easter morn.

Form, reform, and transform my life to welcome the setbacks and successes evangelization always entails.

Grant me the grace to shed the last remnants of willfulness and enter into the core meaning of discipleship.

Let obedience to your truth and your teaching become my chief concern.

Please help me to resist any affection or attachment that threatens my primary love relationship with you.

Amen.

For Reflection

- Recall those times when the Holy Spirit granted you some disclosure of the pointing of Providence, some moment when you saw a glimpse of the path along which your life call was leading you. What was made clear to you? How did it happen?

- How have these glimpses helped you to proceed on the path ordained by God for you?

Chapter 9

Five Building Blocks of Committed Christian Living

What Christ Would Do
Susan Muto[9]

Make me mindful of what Christ would do,
How he would respond on each occasion.
What care and compassion would he manifest?
How can he become the source of my yes?
Yes to the Father,
Yes to the Son,
Yes to the Spirit,
To all Three in One.

This yes is the imprint you've made on my soul,
The flame of love that burns deeply within,
The yes that makes possible the no to sin.
No to the old me
Gives way to the new,
Empty of self, ready for you.

"If you do not stand firm in faith, / you shall not stand at all" (Isa 7:9). The most foundational building block of committed living, the ground level of discipleship, is, in a word, *fidelity* to God's guiding will. Faith in Jesus Christ as our Lord and Savior rescues us from the risk of dissipating our energy in lesser desires that fail to fulfill us. Fidelity to our inmost calling to be and become "another Christ" must stand firm whatever our vocational choice may be. Faith the size of a mustard seed helps us withstand the struggles and focus instead on the blessings associated with our commitment to Christ (cf. Mt 17:20).

The second building block is to *honor* the commitments woven into the fabric of everyday ministry—from selling raffle tickets for a parish fundraiser to helping family members survive a flood. This building block lets us serve the Lord in the duty of the present moment. We no longer see our life as a haphazard collection of disconnected events but as a coherent plan guided by the hand of God. We learn the art and discipline of practicing the prayer of presence in our here-and-now situation.

Trust in God's Spirit dwelling within us is the third building block of committed Christian living. The more trust we have in our Master, the more we are able to resist the uncommitted forces that block the exercise of love and service we owe to God.

"Awe came upon everyone, because many wonders and signs were being done by the apostles" (Acts 2:43). The fourth foundation inserts into our heart the uplifting and lasting disposition of *awe*. It enables us to behold the sacred significance of every person, event, and thing entrusted by God to our care. Awe is a mark of Christian maturity. It softens any arrogant assumption that we can "go it alone." It prevents us from betraying God's call and allows the inspirations of the Holy Spirit to permeate the aspirations of our human spirit.

As we move toward the fullness of discipleship, we sense that we are living and working in a more Christ-formed way. Our renewed commitment to the new evangelization moves us away from a shallow life of complacent belief while gracing us with the courage to meet the challenges Divine Providence places before us.

Being committed to Christ reveals the fifth and final building block we need: the *willingness* to change in order to grow. To do so we must detach ourselves from the tentacles of self-centeredness to such a degree that the bread of our daily responsibility and the wine of our suffering come to fruition in a peace and a joy no one can take from us.

As life moves on from day to day, we soon discover that we are not privy to knowing our call fully nor to predicting what it might entail. When we do become aware of its directive power, we are free to accept or reject what is asked of us, but its full disclosure remains a mystery. Our role is to live in the puzzlement of not knowing while still proceeding on the path God has set for us with its problems and potentials.

Our baptismal call comes alive in a variety of minor and major calls disclosed to us from youth to old age. All reveal something of the consecrated direction our life will take. Beyond these transitory calls stands one that is lasting, one that will influence our life more or less continuously, albeit often in hidden ways. This is the mystery of our deepest life call. It is at the root of the various states of life, positions, or relationships within which we have to express who we are and what we hope to become.

As we move from adolescence to adulthood, we become more keenly aware that the call to commit our lives in one direction limits our availability to move in another. This tension between what can be and what is should not surprise us. It is impossible to become everything we could or would want to be.

The more our spiritual life progresses, the more we are able to behold life as a pattern of providential events. It is not a haphazard collection of accidental happenings. When we stand back and view our whole course at moments of recollection, we see that what is being woven by the divine hand is in dialogue with the gifts and goals evoked by our successive life situations.

Disappointments and failures as well as celebrations and successes are expressions of a divine epiphany. Each happening reaches beyond itself to a mystery of transforming love. In faith we believe that an eternal, loving Mystery guides the world. In hope we trust that goodness will prevail despite evil inclinations and destructive acts. In charity we perceive that nothing happens outside the guidance of an ultimately loving Presence.

At the Last Supper, Our Lord addressed these words of power to his disciples: "You did not choose me but I chose you. And I appointed you to go and bear fruit" (Jn 15:16). The question of who we are called to be is and always will be under the jurisdiction of God. What remains primary is wholehearted acceptance of the invitation to pursue personal holiness; what is secondary concerns how we make this pursuit concrete in accordance with the gifts and talents God gives us.

Let Us Pray

Jesus, you are the Master I am to obey; yours are the attitudes I must imbibe.
Thank you for granting me the grace of sharing in your providential plan as the person I am.

Divine Master, to follow your way is to find my true self; please show me my purpose for being here.

Help me to tread the path that leads to eternal life, and grant at journey's end that my final resting place may be with you.

Amen.

For Reflection

• Consider why responding to the call to commitment holds the key to Christian maturity.

• Has the risk of saying yes to God, despite your misgivings, reaped unexpected rewards? What were they?

• Has fidelity to God's mysterious will for your life bolstered your trust in Divine Providence? Why or why not?

Chapter 10

Adopting the Dispositions of Mary's Heart

Emmanuel
Susan Muto[10]

In my mind's eye
I wonder why
You became God-with-us,
Emmanuel.
Why would you enter
This hell of terror,
Murder, rape,
And every common and despicable
Sin? Surely it was not to win
A following. The cross was no joke,
Yet you took this yoke upon your shoulders
In a gesture of love so audacious
And sublime, it could only be of God.

Perhaps
What attracted you to us
Was the smallness of Nazareth,
That simple place of everyday
Grace, life rife with epiphanies
Of the mystery, a sparrow's
Winged flight, a child crying

In the night, a mother's care,
A father's prayer
Multiplied infinitely.

So that is why,
O Holy Light,
You came to us
One starry night.

"Here am I, the servant of the Lord; let it be with me according to your word" (Lk 1:38).

Mary, whom God chose from the beginning of time to be the Mother of his Son, is the prototype of every disciple called to follow him. She lived in pristine empathy every mystery of Christ's life: his Incarnation, crucifixion, and Resurrection. From her witness to these events, we derive the essentials of discipleship: her joyful and sorrowful life inspires us to excel in faith, never to lose hope, and to love without measure.

Her *fiat* marks a significant milestone in salvation history. The first disposition we must adopt is that of her *faithful* heart. The moment she consented to God's invitation, the Word became flesh. His Mother lived to the full the words her cousin Elizabeth would say to her: "Blessed is she who believed that there would be a fulfillment of what was spoken to her by the Lord" (Lk 1:45).

Mary's *joyful* heart disposed her to run with haste to the hill country to voice the wonder both women shared, saying, "my spirit rejoices in God my Savior" (Lk

1:47). She and Elizabeth felt the stirring of life inside them. They were jubilant. They could not stop praising the Lord. What great things the Almighty had done for them and how awesome it was to remember his mercy from age to age!

Just as Scripture tells us, "If you do not stand firm in faith, / you shall not stand at all" (Is 7:9), so we are told that the joy of the Lord is our strength (see Neh 8:10). Joy lasts when gratification fades away. We enjoy a good meal, but soon we are hungry again. Joy surpasses satisfaction. It prevails when failure replaces success. Joy points to the lasting jubilation that will be ours for eternity. Mary's agony at the foot of the cross gave way to her ecstasy, an experience every disciple protected by her intercession understands.

Thanks to her strong, *suffering* heart, Mary models the virtue of endurance. There was no escape from the piercing sword foretold by Simeon in Luke 2:35. Already, when Jesus was twelve years old, she knew the harsh reality of relinquishment; her Son would have to be about his Father's business (see 2:49). She would have to let him go—all the way from Nazareth to the Mount of Calvary and beyond to the empty tomb.

There is so much about suffering we do not understand. Various ailments, some of which may be terminal, are thrust upon us. We weep over hurts, misunderstandings, and outright persecution. The closer we come to God, the farther away God may seem in those arid, dark nights of the soul; but suffering, as Scripture tells us, has another meaning.

According to St. Maximilian Kolbe, all we need is to turn to the "Immaculata." He says that even the weakest among us, those who have strayed farthest and suffered mightily because of it, can be rescued by their Mother.

As the Apostle Paul confirms: "For this slight momentary affliction is preparing us for an eternal weight of glory beyond all measure, because we look not at what can be seen but at what cannot be seen; for what can be seen is temporary, but what cannot be seen is eternal" (2 Cor 4:17-18).

Every disciple appreciates Mary's *silent* heart. The Gospel records only a few of her words, but every one of them expresses her maternal, faithful, joyful, suffering love. If we sincerely want to follow Jesus, God's Mother will be there to care for us. She is one with the praying Church. She is the perfect model of the person God wants us to be, full of grace and truth and always ready to aid our evangelizing efforts.

Let Us Pray

Gentlest of women, you enfleshed the epiphany of Jesus on earth and brought him to birth.

Make our heart the manger in which your divine infant comes to rest.

You ask us, dear Lady, to radiate your Son's gifts of truth, light, and love to all we meet.

You long to turn us into beams of his sovereign splendor.

You are waiting to intercede for us the moment we tell you our troubles and fears, our hopes and dreams.

God made you the Lady of healings, conversions, and wonders.

Gentle Mother of the apparitions of Christ in our hearts, draw us sinners in imitation of your Son, to reconciliation and sanctity.

Whisper our petitions into the ears of Jesus.

Ask him to help us.

Most loving God, let the virtues you granted Our Lady become in some small way our own.

Know that whatever you will, the gratitude of our hearts will be yours forever.

Amen.

For Reflection

- How often do you proclaim with Mary the greatness of the Lord?

- Do you thank Our Lady daily for accepting her call to be the Mother of God, the caregiver of our Savior and Redeemer?

- What draws you to converse with Mary and seek her help?

Chapter 11

Advancing toward Christian Maturity

Useless Servant
Adrian van Kaam[11]

May I sing to people
About the mystery they deeply are,
About the Spirit in their plodding lives.
Already the fields are white
Ready for the harvest.
But few are the laborers
To gather your chosen ones
In the granary of the Spirit,
To separate the golden grain
Of their graced destiny
From the straw of attachment.
Lord, send me out into the fields
And when I have done all I could
Remind me kindly that I was only
A useless servant.

To advance to Christian maturity, we must return to the teachings of mature Christians. Four saints who model the deepest meaning of discipleship and whom I consider exemplary in this regard are: Bernard of Clairvaux (1090-1153); Teresa of Avila (1515-1582);

John of the Cross (1542-1591); and Teresa of Calcutta (1910-1997).

In one of his eighty-six sermons on the *Song of Songs*, St. Bernard describes the twofold movement characteristic of growing in, with, and through Christ. He calls it "infusion" and "effusion."

For infusion he uses the image of a reservoir, for effusion that of a canal. To mature in Christ means to be filled or infused with his teachings and then, with the help of the Holy Spirit, to control the way we outpour or effuse them to others. He confirms the truth that we cannot give to anyone what we have not first received from God.

Already in the twelfth century, he lamented that in the course of trying to become mature there are far too many "canals" and not enough "reservoirs." Christ exemplified the importance of infusion by going off to a quiet place to pray. Our Lord sets the example we must follow to cooperate with the grace of effusion and to ready ourselves to engage in ministerial activity.

In her masterpiece *The Interior Castle*, St. Teresa says that a complementary condition for following Christ is to be humble by walking in the truth of who we are. This is the virtue that enables us to move from "me, my, and mine" to the mystery of transforming love that is at the center of our being.

St. John of the Cross outlines the essentials of adult discipleship in a short sentence from his *Sayings of Light and Love*. He reminds anyone who would be a follower of Jesus: "Seek in reading and you will find in meditation;

knock in prayer and it will be opened to you in contemplation" (number 158). Spiritually mature Christians know that formative reading of Scripture and the masters perfects their practices of prayer, meditation, and contemplation. They seek the meaning of God's Word for them, meditate upon it, and pray for the grace to act in fidelity to the truth that sets them free. Their aim is to become at one and the same time active contemplatives and contemplatives-in-action.

St. Teresa of Calcutta's story reveals that our thirst for God is like a drop of water in the ocean compared to God's thirst for us. In 1947, on a noisy train transporting her to her annual retreat, she looked at the masses of suffering humanity that would never know the comforts she enjoyed as a nun and a teacher in a girl's school far away from Calcutta. In her heart she heard God say, "I love you. I thirst for you." From that moment on, she took a giant step toward Christian maturity by becoming for the rest of her days a little pen in a mighty hand, caring tirelessly for those abandoned in body and soul, for whom God thirsted.

These four spiritual masters teach us that Christ calls us to first abide with him and then to be faithful to his call to serve others in justice, peace, and mercy in the circumstances where Divine Providence places us. We do not embark on the journey to spiritual maturity to attain consolations, lofty experiences, or signs that we have found favor in the sight of God. Rather we ask the Holy Spirit to give us the courage to be faithful followers, even when our ministry fails to garner success in worldly terms.

This God-centered perspective moves us from timidity to courage. We flow with grace, mindful of what Jesus said to his disciples: "My food is to do the will of him who sent me and to complete his work" (Jn 4:34). We do so by:

1. Fostering the integration of contemplation and action.

2. Seeking, in humility, intimacy with the Trinity as the core of our human and Christian identity.

3. Conforming our will to God's will for us with such a depth of loving surrender that we consent to whatever Divine Providence asks of us, be it in the valley of daily suffering or on the mountaintop of mystical joy.

4. Experiencing the outpouring of God's charity in our hearts and allowing his love for us to be manifested in our love for others.

The more we believe that everything that happens to us has some significance beyond what we see at first glance, the better we may be able to cope with pain and suffering. We can bind our sad hearts to a saving Heart more magnanimous than our own. What appears to be a limit from one point of view can become an opening for meeting divine Love in a surrendered way, filled to the brim with expectation. This meeting is not an escape from reality but the start of a mature spirituality.

Who better than Christ knew to what depths of wisdom and truth hardship and suffering would lead? He chose to accept the cup and to commend his sacrifice to the Father's glory, defeating death and rising victoriously.

Bound as we are to the living heart of Christ, we can share in his Paschal Mystery. It moves us from despair to hope; it guides us from doubt to trust in God's providential plan for us and for all humanity.

At gifted moments on our faith journey, we may find ourselves overwhelmed by needs that draw us like iron filings toward the magnet of God's care. Our longing for help heightens in times of physical stress, emotional confusion, and spiritual aridity. Such weakness is not an obstacle to transcend but an avenue to spiritual maturity.

Jesus cannot coerce this act of trust; it is an invitation we receive to respond to grace and to find meaning in suffering, fully convinced that God hears the cry of the poor and responds to the heartfelt pleas of our fear-ridden self. Now we see as an opportunity for growth what appeared to be merely an obstacle. Now we find, through trial and error, sin and forgiveness, setbacks and new starts, the secrets of Christian maturity.

All the forces that constitute our life—beauty, joy, laughter, disruption, sorrow, sadness—are part of the pattern. Each thread has its purpose in the tapestry of transcendence. Each burden can be a blessing in disguise. The choice is ours: to treat crisis either as a time of closure because of fear or as a time of openness because of faith. The latter choice reverberates with the conviction that suffering can be accepted with hope and courage, not bitterness and resentment. Now is the time to treat ourselves and others more compassionately. Now is the time to accept as providential the limits imposed on us by reality.

The grace of maturing in Christ prevents us from falling into the trap of believing that life is a useless passion or that sadistic forces beyond our control rain suffering upon the innocent. Such negative thoughts need to be banished by frequent acts of abandonment. To face courageously the shadows of pain, to believe that there is light at the end of even the darkest tunnel, are marks of Christian maturity.

The results of abandonment may not be forthcoming at the snap of our fingers. Our pain may persist for a while, but in the process of turning to God, we discover gifts of courage we did not think we had. We begin to understand, if only through a glass darkly, what St. Paul meant when he said with awe-filled abandonment: "It is no longer I who live, but it is Christ who lives in me. . . . I do not nullify the grace of God" (Gal 2:20,21).

Let Us Pray

My Lord, show me the way you have chosen that I may follow.
Let me be one in spirit with those whose steps you have already led.
They left me the message of your way.
Let me hearken to their words.
Let their example soften any hardness in my heart, that I may see the way and follow.
Let me read in a spirit of docility that I may dwell patiently in the darkness of not understanding until your Spirit gives me light.

Your light alone can illumine my darkness.
Let me read with an innocent eye and hear with a trusting ear, that your words may touch my life and transform it wholly.
Lead me, Lord, from the tangled forest of duplicity to the path of simplicity.
Calm my disquiet with your own stillness.
Lift the cloud of egoism from my eyes, lest blinded by pride I lose the way.

Witness my trying, Lord, and when I grow weary, take my hand, whisper direction to my heart, turn my steps toward home.

Amen.

For Reflection

- Recall a time when familiar texts from Scripture or the spiritual classics came alive for you in a new way. What was it in these readings that spoke to your longing and loving heart?

- Can you remember the lingering effect of the inspiration you received?

- What can you do to facilitate further receptivity to such insights both individually and communally?

Chapter 12

Revisiting the Virtue of Hope

You Are Our Hope
Susan Muto[12]

Lord,
Death has no power
To defeat your claim to life.
Out of the soul's abandoned depths
You hear cries agonized:
Is there mercy enough
To comfort our misery?
Is there forgiveness enough
To heal the breach
Caused by pride and perfectionism,
By defeat, depression, and despair?
What words are these
That console a heart
Grown faint with fear!
Come to me. Your burden
I shall carry. Your weakness
Shall become my strength.
Your light dappled with shadow
Shall shine forth like the sun.
My grace is enough for you.

Your words, O Lord, are hope
And consolation, sweet solace,

Oil poured out to soothe
Old wounds, to soften scars,
To turn these dark places
In my soul toward the stars.

Think of the times we have said, "I hope for a good report from my doctor." Or on another occasion, "I have great hope in this renovation of our church." Or referring to a promise made, "I hope to see my college friends this summer."

Common as these experiences are, they do not capture the full meaning of hope. This virtue might better be understood when we dare to say: "I hope that God will give me the grace to deny myself, take up my cross, and follow Jesus" (cf. Mt 16:24). Or "I hope that I will be able to decrease that he may increase" (cf. Jn 3:30). Or "I hope that every worship service I attend animates my soul and draws me closer to God."

There is a distinction between hopes related to events of this world, such as "I hope for a good report from my doctor" and hopes grounded in God, who is not of this world nor affected by it; a hurricane that ruins our hope of going on vacation does not forestall God's sovereignty over the whole world. My own worldly hopes sound more like wishes that I want to be fulfilled, whereas divine hope rests on my belief in the truth of Revelation. It signifies that what I anticipate lies not in what is seen but in what is unseen. Such is the hope that "does not disappoint us, because God's love has been poured into our hearts through the Holy Spirit that has been given to us" (Rom 5:5).

It takes courage to hope "against hope." When we hope *for* something—a reward, an outcome, an assurance of success—our expectations may prove to be obstacles to the fulfillment of God's plan. His plan may be full of surprises we never foresaw, outcomes beyond any we could have imagined.

When we put our hope in worldly plans and projects—in power, pleasure, and possession—we may feel uplifted for a while, but soon this bubble bursts. Unfortunately, our eagerness to bypass the crosses life places on our shoulders, and the hope we harbor to rid ourselves of them, may result in our missing the sense of what discipleship really means.

How, then, might we describe hope in the light of what Jesus teaches? The benefit and beauty of this infused virtue is that it readies us to reject the lie that we can save ourselves. Hope expresses our unshakable confidence in the promise made by Jesus that he will not leave us orphaned (see Jn 14:18). It counteracts the narcissistic expectation that existence has to follow our formulas for fulfillment.

True hope reminds us not to rely on human power, but on the power of God. It gives us the courage to cross deserts of defeat, depression, and despair, and to seek the help we need. It remains as unshakable in desolation as in consolation. Neither scornful pessimism nor condescending cynicism can block the positive thrust of this virtue.

To paraphrase a familiar passage from the Book of Deuteronomy (30:19), substituting for the word "life," hope, and for the word "death," hopelessness, we read: "I have set before you hope and hopelessness, blessings and curses. Choose hope so that you and your descendants may hope, loving the LORD your God, obeying him, and holding fast to him; for that means hope to you."

Think of how hopeful we feel every time we pray that God will pardon our sins, only to discover how much we have already been forgiven. Especially amid crises of transition, when we feel abandoned and alone, hope prompts us to wait upon the Lord and not lose heart. By contrast, hopelessness conjures up attitudes of resigned acceptance of a predestined fate devoid of joy. We fail to see life as a divine adventure released from predictable outcomes and replete with the awesome revelations God has in store for us.

The gift of hope helps us to be faithful to the duties of discipleship in the situations where God places us. Our life becomes at once simple and spontaneous, profound and practical. Placing ourselves before God provides a buffer zone against negativity, hopelessness, inertia, and fear. God's presence grants peace in the face of frustrations, hostility, envy, and distrust. It restores compassion and joy.

Hope yields the benefit of disentangling us from introspective self-scrutiny and preoccupation with imperfection. We see our sinfulness not as the end of hope but as the best reason to place ourselves humbly before the saving love and forgiveness of the risen Lord. He calls us in our weakness not to sidestep responsibility but to work as hard as we can to incarnate Christian values where they are most forgotten.

Hope in the eternal wisdom of God helps us to disclose a style of living that frees us to a large extent from useless, energy-sapping agitation, anxiety, and tension. We find ourselves thinking, feeling, perceiving, and acting more in tune with our divine destiny. Life becomes less dissonant and more consonant. We follow God's direction and learn anew each day how to meet the challenges of discipleship, first of all by praying with the psalmist: "For God alone my soul waits in silence, / for my hope is from him" (Ps 62:5).

Let Us Pray

Lord, preserve me from the panic that ensues when I think of my days as rapidly passing.
Where have the years gone?
What do I have to show for them?

Help me to see the aging process as a gentle passage from action to contemplation.
Let your providential care for my life constitute my fondest hope.
Show me as the years go by the surest path to follow so that one day we may be together in an eternal face to Face.

How hopeful it is, Lord, to be in your presence.
Sharing with you this slowed-down pace fills me with peace.
To see the stars, to feel the sand, to taste the salty breeze—these experiences are too wonderful for words.
Everything is in your hands, myself included.
Whatever happens, let me live in hope that with your rod and your staff you comfort me.

Amen.

For Reflection

• Why is it so important to immediately replace feelings of hopelessness with the assurance of hope?

• In what way does this spiritual discipline make you a less depreciative, more appreciative person?

• What can you do to help others on the edge of despair begin to turn their thoughts and prayers upward to the horizon of hope?

Chapter 13

Where the Seed of Effective Ministry Falls

Reflecting Your Light
Adrian van Kaam[13]

When I ponder things too sublime,
When I put my worth in self-perfection,
In calculation of accomplishment,
Free me from such willfulness
Through the gentle action of your love.
Holy is my life in your presence, Lord.
In you I rise daily
Like Venus from the sea,
Like Phoenix from the ashes.
You are the landscape of eternity
In which my life unfolds
Like a blade of grass after winter's cold.

One of the most beloved parables of Jesus, found in Matthew 13:3-23, begins with the words: "A sower went out to sow . . ."

We can picture him with a pouch of seeds slung over his shoulder. He reached into it to scatter them and inevitably some fell on unfertile soil, bad for growth but good for hungry birds. The seed that settled on rocky ground, if it grew at all, soon withered for lack of roots. Sunshine scorched the shoots, drying them up and retarding their growth. The sower persevered despite the fact that other seeds were choked by thorns. Happily for him, many seeds did fall on fertile soil and produced the good fruit the sower must have foreseen. At a hundred or sixty or thirty bushels, the crop in the long run was a success.

Do we have ears to hear the meaning of our Lord's teaching, or is it as puzzling to us as when he first told this parable to his disciples?

Do we allow the birds of power, pleasure, and possession to peck away at the seeds of humility, purity of heart, and poverty of spirit that characterize followers of Jesus, leaving in their wake nothing but an empty field producing no lasting fruit?

Rocky ground does not offer much sure footing. We end up tripping or we stub our toe and sit on the side of the road feeling sorry for ourselves. The seeds of discipleship planted in us by the divine Sower never take root. We want praise and instead we incur persecution. As far as we are concerned, the Word of God makes too many demands upon us. Before long, we forego its rigor and refuse to leave the rocky road of doubt.

The thorns that shredded the seeds are comparable to those times when we hear God's Word but lack the courage to turn away from alien voices and the anxiety they evoke. A litany of "what if's" soon assails us: What if I lose control? What if I cannot really trust God's plan for my life? What if I am seen as a failure in the eyes of the world?

Another excuse sure to choke the still-small whispers of the Spirit can be an excessive clinging to the "lure of riches." Following the path to inner poverty taught by Jesus means detachment from the illusion that worldly wealth is my ticket to the land of lasting fulfillment. At least there I could see the results of fame and fortune. Poverty may produce little or no recognition. It may mean having to work for less because we decide to put our family and our church first.

The Christian path to liberation begins with renunciation. Our first duty is to renounce whatever separates us from remembrance of our radical dependence on God. The specifics of renunciation may differ, depending on our state of life, but their aim is the same. For the rich, it may be necessary to forego reliance on material possessions; for the poor it may mean giving up resentment of the wealthy. In both cases, excessive attachment to goods or the lack of them clouds our remembrance of God.

Three traits in the life of Jesus deserve our full attention in this matter: his hiddenness, his powerlessness, and his self-emptying. The first trait symbolizes the depth of the relationship between us and God that is hidden from view. It remains for the most part a private matter. It prevents us from boasting about our accomplishments and follows the scriptural imperative: ". . . so that your alms may be done in secret; and your Father who sees in secret will reward you" (Mt 6:4).

The second trait proves that, through human weakness, the glory of God reveals itself. St. Paul says that in this way power reaches perfection: "I am content with weaknesses, insults, hardships, persecutions, and calamities for the sake of Christ; for whenever I am weak, then I am strong" (2 Cor 12:10). The death of Jesus represents the humbling of human power and the triumph of spiritual strength.

The third trait that must become our own is that of Christ's self-emptying. Rather than clinging to his equality with God, he chose the condition of a servant, devoid of any semblance of personal importance. He asks us by virtue of his kenotic love to give up control of our lives and to trust God totally. To empty ourselves means to be the imperfect, finite persons we are—full of concern for our welfare yet willing to take the risk of saying, "Not my will but yours be done." These are the poorest words human pride can utter, yet they ready us to be united with the Lord in a spirit of joy and humility.

The rich soil in which the seeds of God's Word are sown symbolizes our consent to love and serve God and others, motivated not by self-gain but by charity and compassion. We see as infinitely precious every seed of faith God asks us to plant in the arena of evangelization. We begin to understand what the Lord wants us to do and how contrary it may be to our expectations.

The seeds planted in the soil of hidden, powerless, other-centered love grow into trees laden with the fruit of good works. Ours is an abundant harvest radiant with renewed inspiration. Once we may have felt isolated and alone, but not now. On our own and with other members of our faith community, we become seed-planters—which may simply lead in humility to us doing unnoticed deeds like offering others an encouraging word and reminding them how much God loves them. Nothing brings more joy to us than embodying the evangelizing spirit granted to us by the Holy Spirit, in whose light effective ministry always yields an abundant harvest.

Let Us Pray

Lord, teach me the way of detachment
from power, pleasure, and possession.
Help me to attach myself more firmly to you,
Holy Source of life eternal.
Transform my vision so I may see
each finite given as a manifestation
of your infinite care.
The temporal, like a flight of sparrows,
is but a passing moment in the eternal
outpouring of your tender concern.
In my nothingness, let me be present to your
All-ness.
Whenever I grow arrogant,
remind me of my reliance on you.
Temper my worldly cleverness
and fault-finding mentality.
Let my rational intelligence
give way to a sense of wonder—
for who am I that my God should be
mindful of me?
Heaven and earth will pass away, O Lord,
but not your words.
So let me dwell in humble presence
on this directive:
Blessed are you poor,
for yours is the kingdom of heaven.

Amen.

For Reflection

- Do you persist in basing your wellbeing on worldly acclaim rather than growing in the poverty of spirit God intends for you?

- Amid your ministerial plans and projects, are you able to spot the weeds of pride and uproot them before they ruin the good growth God wants to accomplish through you?

Chapter 14

Ministry of Reconciliation

Gentle Vision of Forgiveness
Adrian van Kaam[14]

When I am the brunt of derision
Let me lift my anger in your light.
I need a wider vision.
My sight is narrow,
My feelings twisted.
I cannot see the deeper meaning
Of each event. . . .

However poor, it is this life you love.
Not perfect self-control,
Not phony sweetness,
Not fearful isolation
But an honest response
Of who I truly am.

Now I can hear your invitation
To lift these feelings in your light,
Mellowing my anxious strife
To reach perfection overnight.

I bring my guilt and self-affliction
Before your loving face.
No longer filled with rage,

I feel a wondrous cleansing,
Everything gaining its gentle place
In my vision of your forgiving ways.

All this is from God, who reconciles us to himself through Christ, and has given us the ministry of reconciliation; that is, in Christ God was reconciling the world to himself, not counting their trespasses against them, and entrusting the message of reconciliation to us. So we are ambassadors for Christ, since God is making his appeal through us; we entreat you on behalf of Christ, be reconciled to God. (2 Cor 5:18-20)

The Apostle Paul reminds us that Christ himself modeled what a ministry of reconciliation means, and so must we: "For if while we were enemies, we were reconciled to God through the death of his Son, much more surely, having been reconciled, will we be saved by his life" (Rom 5:10).

Contrary to reconciliation is entrenchment in such deep dynamics of revenge that seeking peace is almost impossible. Christ's redemptive suffering changed that erroneous conclusion "in that while we still were sinners Christ died for us" (Rom 5:8). God so loved the world that he did not hold our trespasses against us. Instead he forgave us, renamed us his friends, and commissioned us to go forth and teach the nations.

The Book of Wisdom describes the awesome event of divinely initiated reconciliation: "For while gentle silence enveloped all things, / and night in its swift course was now half gone, / your all-powerful word leaped from heaven, from the royal throne, / into the midst of the land that was doomed" (18:14-15).

Christ liberated us from evil not by slaying the enemy forces around him but by mounting the cross. On this instrument of torture he reestablished a permanent bond of love between us and God.

Christ enabled us, by virtue of his "crucifying epiphany," to move *from* entrapment in egoism and forgetfulness of God; *through* the "ego-desperation" occasioned by seemingly irreconcilable differences; *to* conversion of heart and a renewed sense of service to others.

To engage in the ministry of reconciliation inwardly, we have to be willing to make peace with layers of conflicting emotions. To mention only a few, there is a battle going on inside us between fear and trust, envy and respect, condemnation and compassion. How can we initiate a peaceful dialogue with others if we allow these tensions to tear us apart?

Outwardly, not a moment goes by when this ministry is not put to the test: perhaps today a coworker offended us by making a snide remark about us in front of our boss, and we responded with defensive tactics that worsened an already volatile situation.

Ambassadors are sent by their country of origin to ports around the world, but how many of them accept as part of their mission being ambassadors for Christ? What might the world look like if we made God's appeal through us a priority?

On a smaller scale, each of us has to bring into our ministry in family, church, and society concerted efforts to be reconciled to God and thereby to engage in effective ministry. Must a family feud go on forever? Does a student have to be combative with a teacher he or she dislikes? Isn't it wiser to agree to disagree agreeably and to try our best to put out the smoldering fires that cause people to burn out? If Christ does not count our trespasses, why do we persist in analyzing everyone in a negative light?

To be ambassadors for Christ, we must let trust in God's providential plan outweigh unreasonable demands for functional performance. We can try to see what is good even in a bad situation rather than wallowing in self-pity and looking for someone to blame.

Reconciliation goes hand in hand with taking time for reflection on the peace and joy of Jesus. To calm our sense of time-urgency, we need to wait upon the mystery that guides us, becoming in the process messengers of reconciliation rather than masters of controversy and condemnation.

St. Paul summarizes the effects of this ambassadorship in his Letter to the Philippians, saying, "Let your gentleness be known to everyone. . . . Do not worry about anything, but in everything by prayer and supplication with thanksgiving let your requests be made known to God. And the peace of God, which surpasses all understanding, will guard your hearts and your minds in Christ Jesus" (4:5-7).

Entering into the circle of love that binds us to the Triune God is always a formative experience. The more we change from within, the more we radiate God's goodness to others. With the help of grace, we find ways to share the gifts we have received with whomever we meet.

The word *shalom* (peace) in Hebrew does not mean cessation of war or absence of trouble. It connotes wholeness, fullness, health—all that makes for humanity's highest good. It means being in harmony with oneself, with other people, and with the world around us—a harmony only possible because we acknowledge a common Source whose benevolent light shines equally upon all creation. For this reason alone, we try our best to respect others and to avoid malicious controversy.

What persons reconciled to Christ and called to discipleship look like can be seen in Colossians 3:12-17 (paraphrased here):

- They clothe themselves with compassion, kindness, humility, meekness, and patience.

- They bear with one another and forgive any complaint issued against them.

- They try to bind all things together in perfect harmony.

- They let the peace of Christ rule in their hearts.

- They are thankful.

- They allow the Word of the Lord to dwell richly in them.

- They teach and admonish one another with wisdom and prudence.

- They sing psalms, hymns, and spiritual songs to God.

- They do what needs to be done in the name of the Lord, giving thanks to the Father for bringing together what no force on earth can wrest asunder.

Let Us Pray

Lamb of God,
Teach me to yield peacefully
To the mystery of your will.
Grant me the wisdom
To be firm without rigidity,
Forthright without harshness,
Forceful without ferocity.

Let the awareness
Of your presence
Instill compassion
In my soul.
As a broken mirror of your love,
Let me share in your forgiving presence
Of my own and others' fragile life.
Fill me with the gentleness of the child,
The meekness of the Lamb.

Amen.

For Reflection

- Would you agree that there is more to the ministry of reconciliation than cessation of conflict or absence of trouble? Why or why not?

- How is it possible to see adversity as an opportunity to grow in peace rather than as an excuse to persist in animosity?

Chapter 15

God's Gift to Every Disciple

Redeemer of the Earth
Adrian van Kaam[15]

Each small thing you daily do
Within the boundlessness of space and time
Holds a dignity and depth of meaning and effect
You can never fully grasp.
When it all becomes too much for you,
Grow serene enough to listen
To the gentle cadence of my voice
In your open, waiting heart.

Always interweave the grace of inner presence
With the ebb and flow of everyday events.
Fight the battle blest against the blight
Of injustice, famine, war, drug-infested streets,
The weeds of sin
On my defiled and desecrated globe.

Don't despair, rekindle hope
In my redemptive guiding light
Restoring dignity in crushed, demeaned humanity
Endowed with transforming potency
By me, Redeemer of the earth.

Spiritual self-direction, God's gift to every disciple, centers on the psalmist's question: "Where can I go from your spirit? / Or where can I flee from your presence?" (Ps 139:7). It invites us to ask in turn: "Do I place my life, with its aspirations and afflictions, under the guidance of the Holy Spirit? Do I accept whatever happens to me as a challenge to discern God's guiding lights?" How often do we wonder, with childlike faith, where God wants us to go?

From youth to old age, our life is like a text written by God that we need to interpret. As we grow in the art and discipline of reading the text of our life, we come to see that God's will is not remote from where we are; it is disclosed in the midst of our life situation. That is why we must not be afraid to ask: "Who am I most deeply? Am I living in fidelity to the vocational call God invites me to fulfill? Where will God's guidance lead me? How can I be a more effective evangelizer amid the routines of ordinary life?"

These spiritually self-directive questions invite us to see ourselves not in isolation from, but in relation to, the guiding light of the Holy Spirit from whom we draw the strength we need to live a virtuous life.

When virtues like patience and perseverance become the lasting dispositions of our heart, they shine forth in our matching character.

Consider the virtue of *docility*. It tempers our fear of the unknown; it lets us go forward into the future despite the uncertainty we feel. Docility makes listening and learning possible. It facilitates durability and determination; it makes us less self-centered and more meek or God-guided.

Docile Christians try to act and speak with thoughtful pauses rather than being pushy and never allowing others to finish their sentence without interrupting. They make every effort to balance gentleness with firmness, meekness with boldness. They try to keep destructive anger in check while reforming the energy behind this emotion to find creative solutions to life's problems. Docility diminishes the inclination to give up in irritation when what we propose does not go our way.

Similarly, the virtue of *detachment* grants us the grace of letting go of superficial concerns and false promises of fulfillment. It frees us from the illusion that our plans have to be God's—or else why should we pray?

With docile and detached hearts, we begin to shift our stance from one of closure to openness. We cease lamenting our limits and instead see them as blessings in disguise.

Paying attention to God's gift of self-direction prevents us from engaging in compulsive, guilt-ridden self-scrutiny. We experience the truth that God loves and forgives the imperfect selves we are. With grateful hearts we pray each day for "the power to comprehend, with all the saints, what is the breadth and length and height and depth, and to know the love of Christ that surpasses knowledge, so that [we] may be filled with all the fullness of God" (Eph 3:18-19).

This experience of intimacy with the mystery of God evokes in us the virtue of *discipleship*, beginning with our acceptance of the commission to become witnesses to Christ in today's world.

The fruit of spiritual self-direction is a gift that keeps on giving. The prejudices, emotions, and assumptions that curtailed our ability to listen and act with docility, detachment, and discipleship no longer have a hold on us. The pull of popular pressures posing as perennial wisdom decreases. What increases is our responsiveness to God's presence and the awareness that the more we rely on God the more we accomplish.

In moments of silent adoration as well as amid active service, we accept as God's gift the universal call to holiness. To paraphrase St. Thérèse of Lisieux from *Story of a Soul*, we learn that living a holy life does not mean doing this or that chore, but fostering dispositions of the heart that keep us humble. Though we are conscious of our weakness, we remain confident in God's goodness to us under all circumstances.

Let Us Pray

Strengthen me, Lord, for the mighty task
Of removing obstacles that block your grace.
Lead my soul into a silence so deep
That only your voice reaches my ears.
Gather my wounded being to yourself
By detaching my soul from earthly desires
That tend to exclude remembrance of you.

In this lifelong endeavor to diminish illusions
Help me endure the dryness I feel.
As I follow you to desert places,
Give me to drink of living water,
Refresh me with your endless graces.

Without your grace to guide me,
I might despair of even trying.
What you measure is not my success
But the tireless effort to struggle onward.

I cannot promise never to resist you.
For ego is not easily tempered.
I can promise that despite my resistance
My love will last with tenacious persistence.
Though mistakes will be made
And detours taken,
Trusting your wisdom
I need not feel forsaken.
The night is dark, the journey long,
But your mercy is there to lead me on.

Amen.

For Reflection

- How have you begun to see your limits as blessings in disguise, as true gifts of God, as graced openings to divine guidance?

- With docility and detachment, consider this question: "What lessons have I learned from my failures personally and relationally?"

- What can you do to help others see with a meek and mild outlook the treasures of meaning hidden in troublesome situations?

Chapter 16

A Formula for
Fully Faithful Ministry

A Glimmer of Your Joy
Adrian van Kaam[16]

Let me dwell daily in your love,
Let it give form to my unfolding.
Let me no longer be the lonely shepherd of my life.
Bring me home from the bracing highlands of the mind,
From the dead end streets in which I shiver in despair.
Shelter my soul tenderly when disappointment hems me in.
Do not allow my soul to grow ponderous and bleak,
Keep alive in me a glimmer of your joy,
Let no adversity defer my course,
Nor defeat my slow advance.
Put a spring in my step, a smile in my heart.
Let me spend this life lightheartedly.
Fill it with verve and inspiration.
Ploughing, we praise; sailing, we sing,
To land on the shore
That teems with your presence.

"The harder I try the behinder I get." Remember that old saying? It suggests that our approach to ministerial stress may be off the beam. We want to rid ourselves of it, to lead tranquil lives, not to be bothered by so many problems. Perhaps it is time to take another approach: to lay this stress to rest by befriending it, to stop fighting our full schedules and learn to accept the challenges placed before us daily without complaints or regrets.

Modern life, from urban sprawl to the smallest village, makes relentless demands upon us. Technology that was supposed to save time costs us more time every day. Once we let go of our naïve expectation that life without any stress would be perfect, we may begin to read the text of daily life with formative wisdom. We may see in it signs of God's providential call.

By entering into the dynamics inherent in every caregiving event, we feel a new sense of accomplishment. Banished are the politics of self-centered cleverness. Befriended is the mystery of binding our gifts and talents to a sustaining presence that shepherds us through the most trying circumstances. Christ forgives our faults. He shows us the way to complete what we started in a gracious and effective manner, full of compassion and self-giving love.

Ironically the distress we feel melts like ice on a warm day when we allow it to disclose the direction in which Christ asks us to go. Just as plants grow stronger when the soil around them is raked and fertilized, so we may bloom where we are planted and advance to new heights of spiritual and social maturity through the stress of ministry.

In seeking such a formula for faithful ministry, we turn to the divine "how to" counsels we find in Holy Scripture. An excellent resource is Paul's second letter to his newly delegated disciple Timothy. In chapter 4, he offers this beloved child advice all followers of Jesus ought to take to heart:

> *Proclaim the message; be persistent* whether the time is favorable or unfavorable; *convince, rebuke,* and *encourage,* with the utmost patience in teaching. For the time is coming when people will not put up with sound doctrine, but having itching ears they will accumulate for themselves teachers to suit their own desires, and will turn away from listening to the truth and wander away to myths. As for you, always *be sober, endure suffering, do the work of an evangelist, carry out your ministry fully.* (2 Tm 4:2-5, italics mine)

In this short passage, there are nine directives, stated by Paul in the imperative. Taken together they offer us the formula to follow to become disciples in this or any age.

The first and most challenging duty we have is to "proclaim the message" in our thoughts, words, and actions. The virtue that most facilitates this honest teaching is "utmost patience." Paul says that the "time is coming"—but for us it may already be here—"when people will not put up with sound doctrine."

The message of justice, peace, and mercy the Lord asks us to proclaim has become increasingly countercultural. What one group sees as justice, another interprets as oppression. Bellicose behavior blankets our planet and outposts of peace come under attack. Such events shadow the proclamation of sound doctrine; they block the ability to hear the truth and let it move from our ears, through our mind, and into our heart.

And yet, in the face of evil, good people still continue to band together to block the life-denying behavior of purveyors of death and destruction. It is true for us, as it was for Paul and Timothy, that inner listening to God's call must never be replaced by "itching ears" that accumulate in selfish ways this or that teaching suitable to one's own desires cut off from the authority of the Church.

Why do we resist listening to Gospel truths? Is it because, thanks in great measure to the proliferation of social media, we can easily "wander away to myths"? Rather than open the Bible, many prefer to consult their daily horoscope.

The second directive is essential: "be persistent." This is the same as telling us to hold on to our promise to proclaim the message Jesus gave us, whether the climate for doing so is favorable or unfavorable. Now is when we need to speak the truth with conviction rather than resorting to unwise accommodation. We must exercise the firmness of admonishment and the gentleness of admiration. In Paul's words, we need both to rebuke and to encourage. There are no hopeless cases, only hopeless people who name them as such. Beyond proclamation and persistence, the formula for faithful ministry requires us to "convince, rebuke, and encourage."

Once we follow these first five directives, we are prepared to obey the remaining four, starting with the need to "be sober." We must never make light of the serious challenges we face. To be sober means to be realistic, not pessimistic. Sobriety is as much a physical decision as a spiritual discipline. It means that we must be prepared to "endure suffering," which is the opposite of self-indulgence. The aim of discipleship is neither to achieve worldly success nor to fear failure but to be faithful to our Lord.

Once these directives become second nature to us, we can "do the work of an evangelist." It takes a lot of preparation to reach this point. We cannot rush the process, since the formation we obtain along the way is bound to be life-changing. Only then can we do what Paul asked of Timothy: to "carry out [our] ministry fully."

Because Paul teaches what he lives and lives what he teaches, he can assure Timothy that this formula for fully faithful ministry will yield the amazing result expressed in these simple yet profound words of the apostle: "I have fought the good fight, I have finished the race, I have kept the faith" (2 Tm 4:7).

Let Us Pray

Good Shepherd, though at times we may feel lost and forlorn, help us to find our way home to the pasture of your presence where happiness reigns supreme.

Crucified, glorified Lord, when stress threatens to become distress, wrap us tightly in your outstretched arms and help us to grow calm.

God of Abraham, Isaac, and Jacob, let us become signs of your covenant of love with a recalcitrant people, always in need of forgiveness.

King of kings, make us worthy to celebrate the paschal feast in the company of your disciples.

Trinity Divine, teach us the way of wonder and gratitude.

Spirit of Love, let us never forget that you are forever calling us home to a new and more abundant life.

Amen.

For Reflection

- Take some time and devise a few concrete suggestions pertaining to ways to live with the disappointments found in every ministerial situation.

- What gives you the courage to persevere in your ministry despite the setbacks you encounter?

- Are you becoming more sensitive to what Christ wants you to do to spread the good news, especially when you are the brunt of disbelief and the object of resistance?

Chapter 17

Gifted by Grace

Responding to Grace
Adrian van Kaam[17]

Responding to grace,
Without hurry or haste,
Means dwelling in you who makes new my day,
Who lessens my fascination with futile ways,
Awakening me to what only remains.

Keep touching me inwardly
Until the light of insight dawns.
Do not allow the flicker of light to die
Before it becomes a living flame consuming me.
Make me treasure the dawn that speaks inaudibly.
Make me cherish the moment of illumination,
Attune me to the tender beginnings
Of grace-filled inspiration.

The words "everything is grace," from St. Thérèse's *Story of a Soul*, give voice to one of the deepest truths of our faith. In John's Gospel, we read of God's only Son from whose "fullness we have all received, grace upon grace" (1:16). In the same vein, the Apostle Paul testifies to the Ephesians, "For by grace you have been saved through faith, and this is not your own doing; it is the gift of God—not the result of works, so that no one may boast" (2:8-9).

As disciples of Christ, we are never ashamed to admit that without God's grace we can do nothing. The words of Jesus to Paul are a source of consolation: "My grace is sufficient for you, for power is made perfect in weakness" (2 Cor 12:9).

It is our weakness that makes the need to ask for God's help our daily prayer. Grace prompts us to trust in the mercy of God, to forgive others as God forgives us, and to choose the way of selfless love. Our actions are not autonomous; they are responses to God's gracious leading.

Grace is about the "much more surely" of God's love for us. It is the unmerited gift that accounts for our redemption: "The free gift is not like the trespass. For if the many died through the one man's trespass, *much more surely* have the grace of God and the free gift in the grace of the one man, Jesus Christ, abounded for the many" (Rom 5:15, italics mine).

"Thanks" is too small a word for this miracle of grace that transcends yet lovingly penetrates our lives: "Yes, everything is for your sake, so that grace, as it extends to more and more people, may increase thanksgiving, to the glory of God" (2 Cor 4:15).

The word "grace" comes from the Greek *charis*, meaning the benevolence shown by the "gods" to the human race. Grace enables us to abandon the illusion that human effort alone can attain our salvation. Gifted by grace, our faith grows stronger, even in the darkest hour.

We are strong because we defer to the strength of Jesus and are perfectly honest about our limits. We stand before God as an open book, hiding nothing of our sins in the blessed assurance that our Redeemer lives. With the Apostle to the Gentiles we say: "Therefore I am content with weaknesses, insults, hardships, persecutions, and calamities for the sake of Christ; for whenever I am weak, then I am strong" (2 Cor 12:10).

According to Paul, the gifts we receive differ due to the grace given to us. The first of them is *prophecy*, meaning that God can commission certain faithful followers of his to go forth and proclaim the good news. Theirs is a work of confirmation, not of prediction. The second gift is *ministry*, whereby the members of Christ's Body care for one another whatever their level of need. The third gift is *teaching* the truth of what Christ reveals to us.

Other diverse members of the one Body, named by St. Paul in Romans 12:8, are: *exhorters*, who defend the faith; *givers*, whose generosity edifies everyone; *leaders* known for their diligence; and *compassionate* hearts, as cheerful as they are helpful.

Grace binds together the many members and lets them function with a vast variety of gifts, which, taken together, accomplish the aims of evangelization. There are many gifts but the same Spirit; an endless cornucopia of services, but the same Lord; a thousand different kinds of activity but the same God, whose grace "activates all of them in everyone" (1 Cor 12:6).

For the common good, one person may speak with the wisdom of experience, another with the knowledge due to impressive learning. The same Spirit deigns that one witnesses to the power of faith and another to the need for healing; still others discern the direction asked of us by the Holy Spirit.

The *chief grace* binding all these gifts together is love. If we do not have love, we are nothing and we have nothing. Charity is the greatest manifestation of God's grace. Without it, no matter how much we do, no progress in discipleship can be made.

Let Us Pray

Lord, grant me the grace of respect for the slow pace of progress your infinite wisdom allows in my life.

Don't let me push beyond borders fixed for me by you from eternity.

Let no hidden hostility disguise itself as zeal for your Kingdom.

Inspire all people of noble purpose to search for means that may diminish the hostility that consumes humanity.

With your gentle grace, teach me how to control aggression rather than being controlled by it.

Transfigure a world of warriors into a band of loving sisters and brothers.

Amen.

For Reflection

- Do you know what your gifts are, and do you try to use them for the good of the Church?

- For what graces do you want to thank God today?

- When you feel weak, are you candid enough to admit it and turn immediately to God for help?

Chapter 18

Traits of True Servanthood

Witness for Your Light
Adrian van Kaam[18]

Like a stained glass window filters
The radiance of the sun in countless color.
Make us light up the corner of the universe
Where we are placed in time and space
Like candles in a dark and empty hall,
Laying down our life little by little
In service of all who pass our way in history.
Let our love be strong and honest
Never a refuge from reality and suffering,
Not sentimental but impeccably right and fair,
So that not we, but you may rise in the heart
Of the multitudes in search of
A shepherd for their lives.

The more we delve into the meaning of discipleship, the more challenging it becomes. How do we move, in anything less than a lifetime, from self-indulgent love to true servanthood? From self-protective falsehoods to friendship with God and others?

The path to follow is so difficult, so full of detours, that we need to find expert guidance. A woman to trust is St. Catherine of Siena (1347-1380), Doctor of the

Church and counselor to countless believing and seeking souls from her time to our own.

In her masterpiece *The Dialogue*, Catherine says that the starting point of the journey to discipleship is none other than the "cell of self-knowledge." For Catherine, solitude is the deepest source of belonging and silence is the fountainhead of truth.

In that cell, the main event that occurs is that we come to know who we most deeply are. This knowledge prepares us to go forth commissioned by Christ to witness to his Word in fidelity to our vocation. Catherine saw the threads of Divine Providence woven into the tapestry of our everyday existence, revealing in due time the grand design intended for us by God.

In this cell of self-knowledge, we experience the encompassing ocean of God's mercy and develop a "holy hatred" for the offenses we have committed. The sorrow of our compunction complements the joy of our resolve not to sin again. We also grow in "true and perfect patience," waiting upon the pace of God's saving grace while pursuing the "virtue of blazing charity," characteristic of disciples wholly conformed to Christ.

This experience of intimate encounter with the Lord illumines us from within and becomes an invitation to unceasing prayer. Now that we understand more of who we are and of what the Lord asks us to do, we can infuse our suffering of the cross, as Jesus did, with songs of praise and gratitude.

As Christ himself says to Catherine in *The Dialogue*: "Have no doubt, my daughter, that I will fulfill your desires and those of my servants regarding what you asked of me. I am your God, I repay every labor and fulfill holy desires whenever I find people knocking in truth and with light at the door of my mercy, so that they may not stray or falter in their hope in my providence."

Christ invites his disciples to progress from being servants of a Good Master to being his intimate friends, a blessing Catherine names "true filiality." She applied this insight by extension to the relationship between a master of formation and a disciple. From the side of the disciple, the main disposition to cultivate is purity of heart. Three principles must be fulfilled to reach this goal. We must be united with God in loving affection, bearing in our memory the blessings we have received from him. With the eye of our understanding, we must see his affectionate charity, how deeply he loves us and draws us to union. Then, if we consider his will first, we can quell our selfish sensuality and approach self and others in charitable service.

The disciple must model the light of Christ's truth and, while offering sound counsel, refrain from judging anyone ultimately, for no one can see the hidden heart but God. Needed here is "holy compassion."

Astute directress of souls that she was, Catherine explained that one ought not confront others with harsh chastisement for specific sins but strive to correct their bad habits, for instance, by showing the efficacy of virtue and the emptiness of vice. She even recommended that we take the vices of others upon ourselves and teach them never to doubt God's generosity.

In line with Catherine, St. Thérèse of Lisieux offered this astute advice. In a letter written on June 21, 1897, to a young priest who asked for her prayers, she said: "Ever since I have been given the grace to understand also the love of Jesus, it has expelled all fear. The remembrance of my faults humbles me, draws me never to depend on my [self], but speaks to me of mercy and love even more." For Thérèse, discipleship consists of "entire filial confidence," complemented by the intent to cast all our faults into the devouring fire of Divine Love.

In the lives and works of these two women, we see lived to the full the disciplines necessary for discipleship: self-knowledge in humility, compunction for sin, patience under fire, and unceasing prayer. Disciples who exude the traits of true servanthood find emblazoned on their hearts this prophetic passage from Proverbs 3:6: "In all your ways acknowledge him, / and he will make straight your paths."

Let Us Pray

Lord, you show me how to meet others where they are.

You relieve their physical and spiritual needs, sparing nothing of yourself.

When it feels to me as if I am wholly spent, be there to uplift my spirit, save me from selfishness, and give me the courage to carry on.

Temper in me the dismissive tendency to do something and be done with it as soon as possible.

Let me find the grace to look beneath the surface appearances of others to their inmost beauty and dignity.

Let me see your face in the poorest of the poor and behold the true worth of the wounded.

Let me mirror with a smile your own appreciation for the souls in need who come my way.

Amen.

For Reflection

- What changes do you foresee having to make so that filial confidence becomes a lasting trait of your commitment to servanthood?

- What way can you suggest for others to alleviate the misgivings that prevent them from trusting in the Lord?

Chapter 19

Four Facets of the Diamond of Discipleship

A Living Message of Gentle Love
Adrian van Kaam[19]

We thank you, Lord,
For your walking on this earth
As one of us.
You were a living message
Of gentle love.
May your love be the center
Around which our life forms itself
Like a shell around an oyster
With its priceless pearl.
Melt all resistance
When your love begins to fashion
Our heart and all its feeling.
Make us sense
The silent stream of love
That flows into humanity
From the mystery of the Trinity.

Think of faith as if it were the power source that propels a car or guides a ship to its destination. Only if we live by faith can we hone in on God's call and detect what we must do to fulfill the destiny chosen for us by the Divine.

Faith is the first and most foundational facet of the diamond of discipleship.

Abraham believed God when he heard the call to leave his country and his kindred to be the precursor of a new nation formed in covenant love (Gen 12:1-3). Later, he accepted in faith that God wanted him to sacrifice his son Isaac for reasons unknown, only to learn that his obedience was sufficient to honor heaven's plan (Gen 22:9-14).

Countless are the times recorded in Holy Scripture when faith dispels fear, confirms the veracity of God's promise, and turns adversity into prosperity. David prevailed over Goliath in the certitude that against all odds God would let him triumph over the giant and save his people (1 Sam 17:50-54). Faith filled empty jars with oil (2 Kgs 4:1-7); restored sight to the blind (Tob 11:7-8); and assured a virgin that her Son would reign over the house of Jacob forever (Lk 1:26-38).

Discipleship risks being reduced to a functional enterprise unless we believe that without God we can do nothing (cf. Jn 15:5). God invites, and we respond—not because we are powerful but because we are powerless. As the Apostle Paul testified to the Romans, "A person is justified by faith apart from works prescribed by the law" (3:28).

In the best of times, faith prompts gratitude to God. In the worst of times, even without proof of belief, faith gives us the courage to fight the good fight and commit ourselves to Christ to the finish (see 1 Tm 6:12).

The stronger our faith is, the brighter will shine *the second facet of the diamond of discipleship*, and that is *the freedom to fail in the eyes of the world.* By the world's standards the cross was the antithesis of success, and yet on that tree hung the Savior of humankind. What endangers discipleship is a calculative model based on the demand for impressive outcomes of functionally generated agendas. According to such a model, affliction makes no sense, yet in Christianity it is exactly such apparent failure that advances our flight to God.

No one better understood this paradox than the Apostle Paul, who wrote, "We are afflicted in every way, but not crushed; perplexed, but not driven to despair; persecuted, but not forsaken; struck down, but not destroyed" (2 Cor 4:8-9).

Only when disciples deny themselves love for power, pleasure, and possession in place of their love for God, can they avail themselves of the grace they need to take up the crosses life sends their way and follow Jesus. Scourged, crowned with thorns, and crucified, he defeated death and lives with us now as our risen Lord.

Disciples whose faith is weak and who do not give themselves the freedom to fail can never mirror *the third facet of the diamond of discipleship*, which is *friendship with the Lord.* He himself announced his intention to move us from the inequality of servanthood to the intimacy of friendly encounter, where God knows us and we know God (see Jn 15:15).

Friends shun superficiality; they stand by us through thick and thin. That is why it was so shocking that Peter betrayed Jesus on the very night he instituted the Eucharist. Unlike Judas, Peter repented. After the

Resurrection Jesus breached the chasm of distrust caused by Peter's betrayal, befriended him to the full, and assigned him to feed his lambs and tend his sheep (see Jn 21:15-17).

The Lord walked on this earth supported by many more friends: those we know by name like Mary, Martha, and Lazarus; those named as his twelve apostles; and those unnamed like the seventy-two disciples he sent forth to proclaim the Word of God.

We serve God by feeding the hungry, visiting the sick, and clothing the naked, but these acts of mercy must go beyond what we do and become bridges to befriending one another because of our faithful, sacrificial friendship with the Lord.

The more these three facets of the diamond of discipleship shine, the more likely it is that we will "bear fruit, fruit that will last" (Jn 15:16). *The fourth facet of the diamond of discipleship is fruitfulness*: it is the result of faithfulness, the freedom to fail for the sake of the cross, and the grace of our having been befriended by God.

What lasts when the world's goods crumble to dust are the fruits of the Spirit. St. Paul names them: "love, joy, peace, patience, kindness, generosity, faithfulness, gentleness, and self-control" (Gal 5:22-23). Opposed to them are the bad fruits of conceit, competition, and envy.

Biblical fruitfulness flows forth from inner transformation of heart. It must not be treated as a measurable entity but as a mystery rooted in God's love for us and our love for one another.

Change of heart leads to the lasting fruit that changes our life and brings to a world darkened by sin the light that shines in the darkness, which the darkness shall never overcome (see Jn 1:5).

Such is the truth of what it means to follow Jesus, summarized in words addressed to all disciples through the mouth of the prophet Isaiah:

> For as the rain and the snow come down from heaven, / and do not return there until they have watered the earth, / making it bring forth and sprout, / giving seed to the sower and bread to the eater, / so shall my word be that goes out from my mouth; / it shall not return to me empty, / but it shall accomplish that which I purpose, / and succeed in the thing for which I sent it. (55:10-11)

Let Us Pray

Lord, you spoke words weighted with truths that do not pass away.

Your words stand fast in the face of evil's defiance of your law.

May my response to forces beyond my control transform a sense of fatalistic surrender into a faithful yielding to the music of eternity.

Give me the courage to cancel from my vocabulary words used to hurt, not heal; to curse, not console; to batter, not bless.

Draw me into those wellsprings of silence out of which words of truth pour forth.

Protect me from people who use words as weapons of abuse, as propaganda to subdue free spirits, as tricks of mental and spiritual entrapment.

Soften the remnants of hardness in my heart so that I may hear and heed your Word, until that day when all words fall silent and I enter into the wordless radiance of your risen presence.

Amen.

For Reflection

- How would you begin to shift your focus from a success model of discipleship to one that witnesses to the paradox of the cross?

- How would you demonstrate to youth and adults that the proof of our faith in Jesus reveals itself in the commitment to bear lasting fruit for our divine Friend's sake?

Chapter 20

Called to be Holy

Death Has No Power
Susan Muto[20]

Death has no power
To defeat my claim to life.
Out of the soul's abandoned depths
You hear my cries agonized:
Is there mercy enough
To comfort my misery?
Is there forgiveness enough
To heal the breach
Caused by depression and defeat?

What words are these
That console a heart
Grown faint with fear!

Come to me. Your burden
I shall carry. Your weakness
Shall become my strength.
Your light dappled with shadow
Shall shine forth like the sun.
My grace is enough for you.

Your words, O Lord, are hope
And consolation, sweet solace,

Oil poured out to soothe
Old wounds, to soften scars,
To turn these dark places
In my soul upward to the stars.

In the account of the Annunciation in Luke 1:35, we are told: "The angel said to her, 'The Holy Spirit will come upon you, and the power of the Most High will overshadow you; therefore the child to be born will be holy; he will be called Son of God.'"

Awe must have overtaken Mary when she heard these words. So profound and full of power were they that we who hear them now gasp in wonder. We ask our Mother Mary to give us the courage to welcome the Spirit of Truth in our hearts and homes. Are we ready and willing, as she was, to let the Most High overshadow us?

The call to holiness beckons us to return to the most basic conditions for fostering awe-filled abandonment to God's will. Whatever our obligations, professionally or socially speaking, whatever our degree of success or failure, wealth or poverty, we come to God as sinners in need of redemption.

On the journey from birth to death, the urgency of time overtakes us. Old habits that cause us to forget God are hard to reform. We can think of a thousand excuses not to pursue a spiritual life, but the price we pay for such stubbornness is high. It is wiser to take a few steps forward, even if we fall several behind; it is better to try and fail than never to try at all. None of us is or ever will be perfect. That is why we cry aloud for redemption.

However pressured we feel by change, however many complaints we voice about the harshness of life and the crowded condition of our schedules, there is no excuse in the long run to remain an hour-a-Sunday-only Christian. We are called to so much more. God is not a harsh judge from whom we must hide. He is the intimate center of our lives. We can resist God's call and stubbornly refuse to listen, or we can surrender to God's waiting embrace. The choice is ours, and it is one all of us must make.

To live in the world but not of the world is to move from inspiration to incarnation, from prayer to participation, from contemplation to action. We grow in holiness when time becomes our servant rather than our being enslaved to its endless tick-tock. We taste the freedom of the children of God when possessions no longer possess us and when we honor our relationships in imitation of Christ and in consonance with our faith and formation traditions.

This integration of prayer and professional activity is the unvoiced goal we seek. Any split between love for the Lord and labor for his Kingdom will need to be healed lest the life goes out of what we do, and we wonder why nothing matters that much to us anymore. Paradoxically, this point of ego desperation may mark a new beginning in our quest to integrate sanctity and service. Too often we blame what is happening to us on outside forces beyond our control. We refuse to look within and face who we are and hope to become. Why can't we find a magic formula for renewal that will resolve these tensions?

Pursuing spectacular solutions is as foolhardy as stagnating in worn-out customs and routines. Neither choice will solve the dilemma that there must be more to life than merely going through the motions.

The solution is in front of us, if only we open our eyes to see it. It means going more deeply into the resources that comprise our Christian treasury of truth. Its wisdom can be found in Scripture, in the writings of the spiritual masters, in our liturgical and sacramental life, and in the time-honored disciplines of silence, formative reading, meditation, prayer, contemplation, and the pursuit of Christian excellence in our ministry.

These resources remind us that holiness is not a private quest for perfection granted to select souls, but rather a universal call issued to each of us. It is not to be equated with ecstatic feelings or extraordinary phenomena. Holiness is loving God with our whole being and radiating that love in every dimension of our life and world. By contrast, if service is insufficiently rooted in contemplative presence, it may lead to arrogance and activism out of touch with our original intention. We work to attain our own ends with little consideration for what God asks of us.

Our decisions and deeds need to be rooted in continual presence to the Divine Presence. Whether we succeed or fail is not the point. What counts for God is our willingness to be serenely present in the world, doing what we can, without succumbing to the ways of the world.

This rhythm of recollection and participation is an essential feature of our agreement to be God's holy people. Whatever we happen to be doing—cooking a meal, writing a letter, teaching a class, nursing the sick—we do it out of love for God and a desire to make this love manifest.

This is what it means to be missioned. Missionary duty is not limited to evangelizing work in foreign lands. It happens day after day in our homes and professions. We may only advance forward inch by inch, but we choose to remain faithful to our Lord, who comes to us without fail. When our weakness is at its worst, that is when Christ's power is at its best (see 2 Cor 12:10).

If Christianity is a religion of the Word, read carefully and reflected upon, it is also an invitation to transform the world into the house of God. We must go into the desert with Jesus, knowing all the while that the test of our growth in holiness will come when we walk with him on the dusty road. Our meeting with him in silence marks the beginning of our lifelong commitment to shout from the rooftops the good news he gives us.

Let Us Pray

Lord, in my quest for holiness remind me to bind every facet of my temporal life to your eternal benevolence.

Let all my actions reflect your unconditional, infinite love for souls and their harmonious unfolding.

Allow me to radiate in childlike trust the light you enkindle from within when I hear and heed your Word.

May I strive to love others with the same love with which I have been loved.

May charity be the hallmark of my appreciative heart, the harbor from where I set sail and the homeport to which I return.

Amen.

For Reflection

- What spiritual disciplines help you to incarnate the universal call to holiness in your personal and communal life?

- In what ways do you try to respond to your evangelical commission from Christ, whether you are married or single; actively involved in ministry or witnessing to a more contemplative life of quiet prayer for the Church?

Chapter 21

Secrets of Successful Ministry

Quiet Me, Lord
Susan Muto[21]

Quiet me, Lord,
Like a child curled up
On its mother's lap,
Like a deer poised
In silent expectation,
Ready to leap at twig's snap
To sheltered safety.
Slow me down
So I can see
Sunrise over spring-green trees,
Ocean's wave splashed upon volcanic rock,
Leaves golden with autumn splendor,
A young man's face, an old man's fingers.
Still the rush
So I can smell and taste and touch
Freshly baked, buttered bread,
Logs bright, burning red,
Birds feeding, kites flying,
All soaring manifestations
Of your mysterious creation.
Let these gifts like cosmic fire
Purify anxious panic.
Lead me, Lord, ever longing

To voiced and voiceless,
Present, praising,
Never ceasing
Prayer.

Believe it or not, these secrets are *silence* and *solitude*.

According to Robert Cardinal Sarah, in his book *The Power of Silence: Against the Dictatorship of Noise*, we must be sure to precede our actions by the practice of contemplative prayer, that is to say, by listening to God and seeking God's will. In other words, we must *be* present to the Lord before we *do* what needs to be done.

Functioning degenerates into functionalism, activity into activism, to the degree that we allow ourselves to become so preoccupied with the weight of accomplishment and the business of the day that we neglect to be still in solitary, loving encounter with our Lord.

This commitment to be with him in silence and solitude readies us to be commissioned by him to go forth from these times of presence to his mystery and to minister in his name. As great saints like Teresa of Avila and Teresa of Calcutta revealed, the fruit of contemplation is the charity that flows from it to all those in need of our love and service.

Silence, both interior and exterior, is a necessary condition for listening with a heart fully attuned to obeying God's will. Solitude, intentional times of aloneness with the Alone, opens us to the transcendent dimension of daily life and reminds us why we must do what God asks of us.

We master in solitude the art and discipline of being *in* the world without being *of* the world. The "Mary" in us resting at Christ's feet must be given priority lest the "Martha" in us becomes a mere functionary instead of a true messenger of the divine.

Like all dictators, the dictatorship of noise wants to curtail our freedom to give priority to the adoration of God and to lead us to choose instead the bondage of distractions. It would plunge us onto the information highway the moment we awaken and fracture our longing for stillness.

Silent wonder that embraces the mysterious silence of God is not a privilege for contemplatives only but a necessity for every disciple. Solitude contributes to our communion with others and with God as well as to our participation in the world.

Solitude is a building stone for the inspirational side of the spiritual life, as is its companion, silence. The life of the spirit can be seen as an intertwining unity of the inspirational and the incarnational. Solitude and silence aid our quest for inner meaning. We are open to the immediate demands of the world, not as ends in themselves but as pointers to the transcendent.

We can never separate the inspirational depth of the spiritual life from its incarnational outflow. While solitude and silence facilitate openness of our human spirit to the Holy Spirit, they also foster and deepen the possibility of our participation in the world.

According to Cardinal Sarah, without silence the work we do can become so noisy and chaotic that it dehumanizes and distresses us. No wonder even the best and most talented servants run out of steam, start to feel chronically exhausted, and need to leave the fast lane and take a breather to lessen the impact feverish activity has upon them.

From this perspective, silence and solitude are not temporary diversions but the secrets of successful ministry. God gives us his Word not in bursts of crashing thunder but in gentle whispers.

In desert moments we discover who we are and what we are to do to advance God's reign on earth. We suspend, at least for a moment, our plans and projects and listen intently to the divine directives God wants us to fulfill. Noise snatches us away from these savings words; stillness insists that we reflect upon them, follow the example of our Mother Mary, and ponder them in our heart.

Contrary to these secret and fertile depths of silence and solitude is talkativeness. We are becoming a population that talks and tweets all the time. Facile speech replaces the thoughtful communication of truth. A person who pauses before she speaks becomes an object of suspicion. We wonder what she is thinking and jump to false conclusions.

Out of silence and solitude come the virtues of sobriety and dignity, prudence and patience. When we wait upon the Lord's guiding grace we become more courteous, while on the other hand, the louder we shout, the less time we have to listen.

A solitary soul, whether in a monastery or in the middle of a family, exudes moderation, knowing intuitively that there is a time to speak and a time to be silent. At first faintly and then with full attention, we hear the music of eternity resonating in each temporal event. Love once meted out in stingy dribbles now extends to the least of these. The deadening effects of living only for ourselves end and we become the fully alive people God intended us to be.

Let Us Pray

Lord, grant that my times of silence and solitude may be sustained by prayer and spiritual reading.

May they mark neither the end of engagement nor the cessation of action.

Rather let them be conditions for the possibility of true participation and communication.

May silence and solitude bind me to my sacred Source.

May my life become a rhythm of inspiration and incarnation, of pondering and participating, of worship and work.

Grant that inner vision and outer action may unite so that I can remain open to the mystery of transforming love made manifest in the simple goodness of everyday life.

Amen.

For Reflection

- Practice attentive silence and prudent solitude this week. In what ways did these practices increase the quality of your communication and the depth of your communion with others?

- Does speaking which emerges from the ground of silence enable you to engage in action that is not impulsive or compulsive but truly reflective and productive?

- What are a few reasons the spiritual masters consider silence to be the ground of authentic speech?

Epilogue

In his Apostolic Exhortation "The Joy of the Gospel," Pope Francis says that "one of the more serious temptations which stifles boldness and zeal is a defeatism which turns us into querulous and disillusioned pessimists, 'sourpusses'" (paragraph 85). This is quite an accusation! He goes on to say that none of us can go off to battle unless we are fully convinced of victory beforehand: "If we start without confidence [and joy], we have already lost half the battle and we bury our talents." We forget Christ's promise that his grace is sufficient for us, and that our power is made perfect in weakness (see 2 Cor 12:9).

What, then, must we do to not be accused of being a "sourpuss"?

First of all, we must avoid at every turn the false paths to fulfillment identified by Pope Francis. Among others, these are self-centered subjectivism, consumerism, joyless judgmentalism, sentimental emotionalism, excessive activism, defeatism, and the loss of hope.

The only way to follow Jesus to the finish line of faith is to abandon ourselves without reservation into the hands of God. The "revolution of tenderness" (paragraph 88) to which the Holy Father calls us begins when we surrender to God like little children who sleep without fear in their Father's arms.

To overcome joyless self-indulgence is to grow closer to Jesus day by day. The more we accept without complaint the small nothings we are obliged to do, the holier we become. We listen to the soft cadence of God's call in our heart and in our surroundings and make its rhythms our own.

Total trust in the unconditional love of God for us is a sure cure for complacency and chronic complaining. God is there to help us when we fall and to encourage us to go on when we feel like giving up. There is no room for despair when one possesses this much trust. Despite whatever shadows appear in our life, Christ follows the law of love , says Pope Francis. For us this means to "pray for a person with whom I am irritated [because this] is a beautiful step forward in love, and an act of evangelization" (paragraph 101).

Evangelical joy partners with an unshakable simplicity of spirit that encourages us to obey God's loving will for our lives. We are wayward children called to return to the house of our Father. If we forfeit the joy that gives our life meaning, we may soon find that our work has no savor.

The witness of the saints and scholars we have met in this book inspires us to move from a fragmented life to an integrated one guided by God. This attitude of gratitude, with Christ as our guide, lets seeds of discipleship planted in our hearts by the Lord grow to full and lasting maturity.

Let me close with these words of Pope Francis:

The good news is the joy of the Father who desires that none of his little ones be lost, the joy of the Good Shepherd who finds the lost sheep and brings it back to the flock. The Gospel is the leaven which causes the dough to rise and the city on the hill whose light illumines all peoples. (paragraph 237)

Notes

1. *Readings from A to Z: The Poetry of Epiphany*, Susan Muto, co-author (Pittsburgh, PA: Epiphany Association, 2000), 14-15.

2. *The Roots of Christian Joy* (Denville, NJ: Dimension Books, 1985), 132-133.

3. *The Woman at the Well* (Pittsburgh, PA: Epiphany Books, 1993), 50.

4. *The Commandments: Ten Ways to a Happy Life and a Healthy Soul*, Susan Muto, co-author (Ann Arbor, MI: Servant Books, 1996), 211.

5. *The Commandments*, 36-37.

6. *The Woman at The Well*, 79.

7. *Divine Guidance: Seeking to Find and Follow the Will of God*, Susan Muto, co-author (Pittsburgh, PA: Epiphany Association, 1994), 55.

8. *Divine Guidance: Seeking to Find and Follow the Will of God*, 127.

9. *Readings from A to Z: The Poetry of Epiphany*, 80.

10. *Readings from A to Z: The Poetry of Epiphany*, 63-64.

11. *Readings from A to Z: The Poetry of Epiphany*, 45.

12. *Meditation in Motion: Finding the Mystery in Ordinary Moments* (Pittsburgh, PA: Epiphany Association, 2001), 96-97.

13. *Readings from A to Z: The Poetry of Epiphany*, 37.

14. *Divine Guidance: Seeking to Find and Follow the Will of God*, 94.

15. *Divine Guidance: Seeking to Find and Follow the Will of God*, 55.

16. *Growing through the Stress of Ministry*, Susan Muto, co-author (Totowa, NJ: Resurrection Press, 2005), 84.

17. *Divine Guidance: Seeking to Find and Follow the Will of God*, 181.

18. *Practicing the Prayer of Presence*, Susan Muto, co-author (Mineola, NY: Resurrection Press, 1980), 113.

19. *Practicing the Prayer of Presence*, 114.

20. *Readings from A to Z: The Poetry of Epiphany* (Pittsburgh, PA: Epiphany Association, 2000), 62.

21. *Meditation in Motion: Finding the Mystery in Ordinary Moments*, 108-109.

Recommended Reading

- Adrian van Kaam. *Divine Guidance: Seeking to Find and Follow the Will of God* (Pittsburgh, PA: Epiphany Association, 1994). (Co-authored with Susan Muto).

- Mother Teresa. *Essential Writings* (Maryknoll, NY: Orbis Books, 2005).

- Susan Muto. *Gratefulness: The Habit of a Grace-Filled Life* (Notre Dame, IN: Ave Maria Press, 2018).

- Adrian van Kaam. *Growing through the Stress of Ministry* (Totowa, NJ: Resurrection Press, 2005). (Co-authored with Susan Muto).

- Susan Muto. *Meditation in Motion: Finding the Mystery in Ordinary Moments* (Pittsburgh, PA: Epiphany Association, 2001).

- Adrian van Kaam. *Practicing the Prayer of Presence* (Mineola, NY: Resurrection Press, 1980). (Co-authored with Susan Muto).

- Adrian van Kaam. *Readings from A to Z: The Poetry of Epiphany* (Pittsburgh, PA: Epiphany, 2000) (Co-Authored with Susan Muto).

- Bernard of Clairvaux. *Selected Works* (New York: Paulist Press, 1987).

- Thérèse of Lisieux. *Story of a Soul*, trans. John Clarke (Washington, DC: ICS Publications, 3rd edition, 1996).

- *The Collected Works of St. John of the Cross*, trans. Kieran Kavanaugh and Otilio Rodriguez (Washington, DC: Institute of Carmelite Studies, 1991).

- *The Collected Works of St. Teresa of Avila, Volume 2: The Way of Perfection*, trans. Kieran Kavanaugh and Otilio Rodriguez (Washington, DC: Institute of Carmelite Studies, 1980).

- Adrian van Kaam. *The Commandments: Ten Ways to a Happy Life and Healthy Soul* (Ann Arbor, MI: Servant Books, 1996). (Co-authored with Susan Muto).

- Catherine of Siena. *The Dialogue*, trans. Suzanne Noffke, (New York: Paulist Press, 1980).

- Robert Cardinal Sarah. *The Power of Silence Against the Dictatorship of Noise* (San Francisco, CA: Ignatius Press, 2017).

- Adrian van Kaam. *The Roots of Christian Joy* (Denville, NJ: Dimension Books, 1985).

- Adrian van Kaam. *The Woman at the Well* (Pittsburgh, PA: Epiphany Books, 1993).

- Susan Muto. *Virtues: Your Christian Legacy* (Steubenville, OH: Emmaus Road Publishing, 2014).

About the Author

Susan Muto, Ph.D., is executive director of the Epiphany Association, based in Pittsburgh, Pennsylvania, and dean of the Epiphany Academy of Formative Spirituality. She holds a doctorate in English literature from the University of Pittsburgh, where she specialized in the work of post-Reformation spiritual writers. From 1966 to 1988, she served in various administrative and teaching positions at the Institute of Formative Spirituality (IFS) at Duquesne University.

Dr. Muto has been teaching the literature of ancient, medieval, and modern spirituality for over forty years. Her writings include companion texts to the masterpieces of St. John of the Cross. Her latest book is *Gratefulness: The Habit of a Grace-Filled Life* (Ave Maria Press, 2018). She has also recorded popular audio series. All of these resources are available through the Epiphany Association (www.epiphanyassociation.org).

Her articles have appeared in *Catholic Digest, Mount Carmel, Pittsburgh Catholic*, and *Human Development*. She has written more than forty books, many of them co-authored with Fr. Adrian van Kaam. She lectures internationally on the Judeo-Christian formation tradition.

In 2014 she received the Aggiornamento Award presented by the Catholic Library Association in recognition of an outstanding contribution made by an individual or an organization to the ministry of renewal modeled by Pope St. John XXIII.

New City Press

New City Press is one of more than 20 publishing houses sponsored by the Focolare, a movement founded by Chiara Lubich to help bring about the realization of Jesus' prayer: "That all may be one" (John 17:21). In view of that goal, New City Press publishes books and resources that enrich the lives of people and help all to strive toward the unity of the entire human family. We are a member of the Association of Catholic Publishers.

www.newcitypress.com
202 Comforter Blvd.
Hyde Park, New York

Periodicals
Living City Magazine
www.livingcitymagazine.com

Scan to join our mailing list
for discounts and promotions
or go to www.newcitypress.com
and click on "join our email list."